THE SELECTED POEMS OF

Howard Nemerov

THE
SELECTED
POEMS OF
Howard

Edited by
Daniel Anderson

Foreword by
Wyatt Prunty

Swallow Press
Ohio University Press
Athens

Nemerov

Swallow Press/Ohio University Press, Athens, Ohio 45701
© 2003 by Swallow Press/Ohio University Press
Printed in the United States of America

The poems in this volume have appeared in the following earlier collections:

The Collected Poems of Howard Nemerov, The University of Chicago Press, 1977,
© 1977 by Howard Nemerov; *Sentences,* The University of Chicago Press, 1980,
© 1980 by Howard Nemerov; *Inside the Onion,* The University of Chicago
Press, 1984, © 1984 by Howard Nemerov; *War Stories,* The University of
Chicago Press, 1987, © 1987 by Howard Nemerov; and *Trying Conclusions,*
The University of Chicago Press, 1991, © 1991 by The University of Chicago.

Swallow Press/Ohio University Press books are printed on acid-free paper ∞ ™

11 10 09 08 07 06 05 04 03   5 4 3 2 1

Library of Congress Cataloging-in-Publication Data

Nemerov, Howard.
    [Poems. Selections]
    The selected poems of Howard Nemerov / edited by Daniel Anderson ;
foreword by Wyatt Prunty.
        p. cm.
    ISBN 0-8040-1059-5 (alk. paper) — ISBN 0-8040-1060-9 (pbk. : alk. paper)
    I. Anderson, Daniel, 1964– II. Title.

PS3527.E5A6 2003
811'.54—dc21

                                                    2003042380

Contents

Foreword

Howard Nemerov was a wonderfully engaging friend, but in print and in the classroom he could be aloof, even austere. He said of himself that he tended to hit young poets on the head so they never did *that* again. Anyone teaching a poetry writing workshop with Howard needed to know triage. But Howard's arena was ideas, where he made no compromises. There his interlocutors ranged from Lucretius to Owen Barfield, God to Ann Landers, Aquinas to ET, and Augustine to Heisenberg and Planck or Albrecht von Haller, whom Nemerov quoted as follows: "Nature knits up her kinds in a network, not in a chain; but men can follow only by chains because their language can't handle several things at once." Aware of the limitations of language, Nemerov developed a set of figures that knitted networks of meaning for him and became the essential vocabulary for his poetry. These were the seeds, trees, streams, birds, mirrors, snowstorms, and seasonal changes of his most earnest contemplation. Because, as Nemerov said, thought proceeds by dividing, some mode of knitting was essential, and figures did that nicely. The word "ravel," used in "Painting a Mountain Stream," is key to understanding Nemerov. Just as figures simultaneously reveal and conceal, so any process—stream, season, thought, generational change—will ravel, will join and fray at once.

Nemerov was a skeptic in dialogue with hope. He cast a longing eye toward neoplatonism, window-shopped the Aristotelian aspects of Aquinas, but ended up viewing America's midcentury suburbs through the lens of process philosophy, where formulas were more reliable than forms and the logos was more verb than noun. Or as Nemerov says in "The Loon's Cry,"

> I thought I understood what that cry meant,
> That its contempt was for the forms of things,
> Their doctrines, which decayed—the nouns of stone
> And adjectives of glass—not for the verb
> Which surged in power properly eternal

Against the seawall of the solid world,
Battering and undermining what it built[.]

What Aquinas meant by *potentia* Nemerov found visible in the guise of trees, seeds, snow, running water, and seasons, each of these figures more significant for the change it entailed than for the form it inhabited. And Nemerov's view of this led him to certain conclusions. "We live in two kinds of thing," he announces toward the end of "The View from an Attic Window." First there are "The powerful trees, thrusting into the sky / Their black patience." Their "branching / Relation teaches how we endure and grow." Second there is "the snow," a figure for what enables potentia, the vast multiplicity of our kind that lets us evolve into the future but in Nemerov's view means loss of individual significance.

The same vision informs "A Spell before Winter," where Nemerov says, "I speak to you now with the land's voice, / It is the cold, wild land that says to you / A knowledge glimmers in the sleep of things." Still on the subject of dormancy and individual loss, in "Again" Nemerov bells out,

Again, great season, sing it through again
Before we fall asleep, sing the slow change
That makes October burn out red and gold
And color bleed into the world and die[.]

Every beginning entails an end, but between these two extremes things can be beautifully complicated.

In "Painting a Mountain Stream," process and potentia are figured by running water, and the focus is on the way we take that which is ongoing and make it static in order to understand it. "Running and standing still at once / is the whole truth," Nemerov begins. Then he concludes, "paint this rhythm, not this thing." The dynamic Nemerov has in mind ravels the world with seasonal loss and return, generational loss and renewal. Meanwhile, as we are told in "The Blue Swallows," our knowledge of all this is restricted to "shapes invisible and evanescent" even as we struggle to "Weave up relation's spindrift web." One "web" of "relation" we "weave" is religion, but there Nemerov balked.

Of Christian hope Nemerov liked to say that as a good Jew he couldn't respect a God who was sentimental about what his people did. Nemerov was full of theological sass, and in that medium was as serious as he was irreverent. "Acts of God," he stated, in a poem of that title, "Are exhibitions of bad taste on a scale / Beyond belief." Of faith and mortality he said, in "Facing the Funerals," "Men have their faiths as coffins have their handles / Needed but once but handy to have then." For Nemerov, the afterlife was a perennial object of debate, if not belief. It was a hope to be batted over the locutionary net, a pursuit whose charm derived more from the motion of thought than from any conclusions drawn.

Nemerov's backtalk to God made special use of the shortcomings of theology. Howard never tired of the irony of Dante's placing Eve, the one to whom we owe our mortality, in the hierarchy of the blessed at the end of the *Paradiso*. What for some was the *felix culpa* garnered only irony for Howard. At the same time, however, Nemerov never quit worrying such issues. It was at the opening of the first Sewanee Writers' Conference in 1990, where Howard, the inaugural reader, thinking of his long association with Sewanee and Sewanee's long association with the Episcopal Church, began by saying he was an agnostic Jew but that there had to be something to religion "for a place to be as kind as this one." Then, looking off in the direction of the Seminary's portion of the campus, he observed that "without God life would not be serious," and added, "and without theology it would not be nearly so funny."

It seems that Howard read what Aquinas had to say about potentia, yoked that with what modern physics and linguistics had to contribute concerning indeterminacy, and, though he disliked him immensely, borrowed Martin Heidegger's notion that being is more verb than noun, then proceeded to write a life's worth of responses. There was a certain amount of gnostic pride in this, but it was balanced by a skeptic's humility. Writing an introduction for Owen Barfield's *Poetic Diction: A Study in Meaning*, Howard suggested that America's recurrent outbreaks of "modernism" always seem to see themselves as "anti-romantic" but quickly reveal themselves to be "variation[s] on superficial aspects of the Romantic movement, while something submerged and unfinished about that movement remains largely untouched." In the "submerged and unfinished" one may find T. E. Hulme's characterization of romanticism as "spilt religion." But Alfred North Whitehead's term "scientific materialism" comes closest to the question as Nemerov framed it. Chaos was always just under the surface of the world's order, as in "Striders," where water bugs "walk atop the water's thinnest skin" and are continually threatened with drowning, or in "Poetics," where we are told that the "story" that makes sense of our lives is a "set of random accidents redeemed / By one more accident, as though chaos / Were the order that was before creation came." The question for Nemerov was which had primacy, the imagination, as Wallace Stevens would argue, or "a universe of independently and fatally moving *things*," as Nemerov uneasily suspected. Wishing this *either/or* did not exist, the speaker in Nemerov's "The Loon's Cry" says,

> I envied those past ages of the world
> When, as I thought, the energy in things
> Shone through their shapes, when sun and moon no less
> Than tree or stone or star or human face
> Were seen but as fantastic Japanese
> Lanterns are seen, sullen or gay colors
> And lines revealing the light that they conceal.

Some higher order imminent in nature remained a desire if not real hope for Nemerov, a beautiful proposition worth rehearsing if not believing. Perhaps another bit of unfinished Romantic business, it nevertheless was the impetus for poems. Resolution to this desire was found in the poet's constitutive act of naming one thing by the properties of another, a "respeaking" that is "the poet's act." Thus at the conclusion of "The Loon's Cry" a train's whistle and a bird's cry become one in the speaker's act of renaming and reordering experience.

Nemerov's poem "Figures of Thought" shares its title with an essay that is the title piece to a collection of essays. In both instances Nemerov considers the ways certain shapes ("not obvious, / Not inaccessible, but just between") are ciphers for "the beautiful / In Nature." The kind of meaning knitted in this poem becomes evident as soon as we consider that a cipher is a naught or zero, a nonentity, secret writing, a code or the key to a code, an intricate weaving of letters, or, as the verb to cipher, the solving of problems or practice of secret writing. Nemerov intends all of these, as our "dry delight" derives from mediating between what in the cipher-like figure is at once both hidden *and* revealed. Also there is what Nemerov's figures preserve for us to study, as in the case of the seeds described in "A Cabinet of Seeds Displayed," which begins, "These are the original monies of the earth." What the seeds instruct is that "all economies are primitive," but by their "reservations" and our "contemplation" of them they have the ability to "teach / Our governors, who speak of husbandry / And think the hurricane, where power lies." Howard Nemerov understood the medieval distinction between power and force, and he found that philosophical principle alive in the world around him.

For Nemerov a figure not only disguises and reveals at once, it embodies an essential truth about our condition. Meaning derives from the play between what is hidden and what is revealed. The conversational tone at one point in a Nemerov poem and a rhetorical flight at another typically are part of this play. The hermeneutical gamesmanship in Nemerov's aesthetic is different from more static uses of the image. The truth of a Nemerov poem is lived in the aggregate of what the poem does, with a skeptic's questions pitted against figures of hope, or, less than that, then those questions pitted against figures whose implications exceed the terms of such questions. Nemerov says in "Runes" what he frequently tells us elsewhere, in "Holding the Mirror Up to Nature" and "The Human Condition," for example. He tells us that his "theme" is

> . . . of thought and the defeat
> Of thought before its object, where it turns
> As from a mirror, and returns to be
> The thought of something and the thought of thought,
> A trader doubly burdened, commercing
> Out of one stillness and into another.

Meaning in Howard Nemerov's poetry emerges from the struggle between limit and imaginative free play, the given condition of the "defeat / Of thought" and the mysteries of thought's "object" respoken by a poem. By using figures, Nemerov battles the fact that "men can follow only by chains because their language can't handle several things at once." The figures Nemerov's poetry uses most often—seeds, trees, snow, birds, mirrors, running water, seasons—are where limit, in the form of our mortality, struggles with our imaginative power to see something more. For example, despite our mortality the "infantile hope / That" a life's road "ends but as the runway does," as Nemerov proposes in "Trying Conclusions," the title poem to his final collection. Reading Nemerov's poetry, the imaginative task becomes ours, as a poem turns out to be a double hermeneutic—an interpretation of experience for the poet and an interpretation of utterance for the reader. Meanwhile the poem lives only when the reader becomes its instrument, its reoccasioned mind and voice. Howard Nemerov knew this, as he understood that the final task of "respeaking" is left to the reader.

In commending to the reader the wise selection of Nemerov poems contained in this volume I should add that there is another basis upon which Howard Nemerov's poetry achieves its meaning, and that is by aesthetic wholeness. Nemerov did not write for musical effect. In fact he frequently cautioned against poets who intoned their poems when they read. But Nemerov did think musically in the sense that his poems enjoyed a wholeness of perspective and auditory control that one associates with melody. What I would commend, therefore, is the poetry of one of our greatest talents who spent a lifetime refining his technique. Talent itself is a litmus test for authority. That Nemerov also chewed the gristle of some of the toughest intellectual problems facing late modern poets only adds to the accomplishment gathered in the following pages. What the reader will find here is a struggle in which the aesthetic triumph of Nemerov's poetry renames and thus reorders the threats of scientific materialism and a century of unprecedented violence. The drama here is nothing less than that of the human spirit pitted against human experience.

Wyatt Prunty

Preface

By the time of his death in July of 1991, Howard Nemerov had pro-
duced three novels, two collections of short stories, six volumes of
criticism, and thirteen books of poetry. His fourteenth collection,
Trying Conclusions: New and Selected Poems, 1961–1991, appeared
from his longtime publisher, the University of Chicago Press, in the
fall of 1991. That same year the University of Missouri Press printed
A Howard Nemerov Reader. Nemerov held the post of consultant
in poetry for the Library of Congress (1963–64). He won both the
Pulitzer Prize and the National Book award in 1978 for *The Collected
Poems.* He was a recipient of Yale University's Bollingen Prize, the
first Aiken Taylor Award for Modern Poetry from the *Sewanee
Review,* and the National Medal of the Arts. Beginning in 1976,
Nemerov served as a chancellor for the Academy of American Poets,
and from 1988 to 1990, he was the Poet Laureate of the United States.

Howard Stanley Nemerov was born on March 1, 1920. He grew
up in New York City, where his parents, David and Gertrude, were
the proprietors of a clothing and fur business. Two of their three
children would pursue careers in the arts; one of Howard's sisters was
the photographer Diane Arbus, who was known for her disturbing
portraits. Her subjects included, among others, dwarfs, giants, twins,
nudists, and the bizarre inhabitants of Coney Island. Arbus, for
whom Nemerov wrote the poem "To D——, Dead by Her Own
Hand," ultimately took her own life in July 1971.

After graduating from Harvard in 1941 with an A.B., the high-
est degree he would earn, Nemerov flew with the Royal Canadian
Air Force in World War II from 1942 to 1944, then became a first
lieutenant in the U.S. Army Air Forces, serving from 1944 to 1945.
In 1946, he began a life in teaching that would span nearly forty-five
years, holding appointments at Hamilton College, Bennington Col-
lege, Brandeis University, the University of Minnesota, and Hollins
College. He finally arrived in 1969 at Washington University in St.
Louis, where he would spend the rest of his academic career, first as
a visiting Hurst professor (1969–70), then as professor of English

from 1970 to 1976, and ultimately as Edward Mallinckrodt Distinguished University Professor of English.

If the poems of Howard Nemerov frequently reflect the mind of one who spent his entire professional life teaching, they accomplish this in the best sense of the term "academic." They delight in wisdom, and revel in poetry's original task of naming. As a writer who was also an academic, however, Nemerov rejected the solipsism and pretentiousness that has come to characterize so many poems written today. He scrapes the surface of this state of the art in his wicked epigram "On Being a Member of the Jury for a Poetry Prize":

> *Jury's* the *mot juste,* under our ground rules:
> I may say guilty and I mostly do,
> But sentencing's beyond me, poeticules,
> As, by your poems, it's beyond most of you.

"Poetry is a way of getting something right in language," Nemerov remarks in his essay "Poetry and Meaning." "For the lover of poetry would never have become a lover of poetry, much less a student of poetry, had he not at first had this feeling of rightness and certainty about some piece of language." Perhaps over the years this "feeling of rightness" has become increasingly subjective to poet and reader alike. For Howard Nemerov, though, who liked to say, "Write English, not English Department," the standards for clarity and accuracy were always high. He believed, as do the best of poets, that language not only can but should aspire to replicate the splendors of the physical world, and in Nemerov's poems there is a precision, both wise and patient, that quietly condemns linguistic carelessness. We encounter this exactitude, for instance, in poems such as "For Robert Frost, in the Autumn, in Vermont," where "All on the mountains, as on tapestries / Reversed, their threads unreadable though clear, / The leaves turn in the volume of the year[,]" and in "The Statues in the Public Garden," where "The weather-beaten famous figures wait / Inside their basins, on their pedestals, / Till time, as promised them, wears out of date."

In "A Defence of Poetry," Shelley writes that the language of poets is metaphorical, and "it marks the before unapprehended relations of things and perpetuates their apprehension[.]" He also maintains that "All high poetry is infinite; it is as the first acorn, which contained all oaks potentially." The first assertion submits that poetry is a manner of thinking, and we see this in Nemerov's poetry as he mines the figurative richness of everyday things—a snow globe, goldfish, trees, the seed, the town dump—and apprehends a pathos in the most pedestrian of objects. The latter observation, that poetry "is as the first acorn," is a conceit for which Nemerov has a great affection. Though Shelley was speaking in the broader context of a poetic tradition, Nemerov embraces the metaphorical essence of his phrase, and finds in it a compelling contradiction to which he often returns. "This is about the stillness in moving things," he begins "Runes":

> In running water, also in the sleep
> Of winter seeds, where time to come has tensed
> Itself, enciphering a script so fine
> Only the hourglass can magnify it, only
> The years unfold its sentence from the root.

In *The Well Wrought Urn,* Cleanth Brooks argues, and partially laments, that "[our] prejudices force us to regard paradox as intellectual rather than emotional, clever rather than profound, rational rather than divinely irrational[,]" and yet he concludes that paradox "is the language appropriate and inevitable to poetry." For Howard Nemerov, paradox was not merely an exercise in cerebral recreation, but a state of being, one in which he found, simultaneously, joy and sorrow, beauty and death, potential and decay. Such philosophical meditations in poetry commonly run the risk of veering into bloodless abstraction, but Nemerov never lost sight of the fact that he was writing for someone other than himself (writing, too, for someone other than poets). As a result his ruminations transcend intellectual musing; they are human. Even while his poems offer us a highly intelligent, figurative synthesis of the world before the poet's ken, it is not beneath him to pause and remind us that the currencies of knowledge and genius—beauty, too—have their foundations in the smallest of denominations, that "from the alphabet come Shakespeare's Plays, / As from the integers comes Euler's law."

At a time when no small number of his contemporaries were

taking an increasingly pyrotechnic approach to language, advancing
a thematic agenda of greater emotional openness, and weaving their
individual identities into the fabric of poetry, Nemerov pursued an
aesthetic in which intellectual curiosity (not to be confused with
snobbery or pretentiousness), wit, empathy, music, and accessibility
were the mainstays of his verses. In *Journal of the Fictive Life*, origi-
nally published in 1965, Nemerov glibly recalls, "I remember a poet's
writing to me several years back, You are at present the most under-
rated poet in the country. But then, he added, that's better than
being the most overrated poet in the country. I was and remain im-
pressed by the short distance between the two extremes." There has
never been a shortage of poets willing to be overestimated, and it is
not uncommon for some to compensate with flamboyance and affec-
tation for what they lack in craft and talent. But Howard Nemerov
sustained a quiet, ironic, and meditative drive in his poems through-
out his career, even as the landscape of poetry grew ever more exotic.

More than a decade after his death, this book is intended to rep-
resent the range of Howard Nemerov's virtues as a poet—his wry wit,
his attentive eye, his capacity for marking "the before unapprehended
relations of things." In this collection also are some of the most res-
onant and authoritative iambic lines written in American poetry in
the second half of the twentieth century. Whether he happened to be
punctuating an epigrammatic thought, or building and sustaining
the mournful cadences of poems such as "The Pond," "The Loon's
Cry," and "The Dying Garden," Nemerov rarely failed to capitalize
on the power of blank verse.

He once wrote that if a poet "does his work properly, there
won't be any other name for the situation (and for his being in it)
than the one he invents, or, rather, his name will swallow up all
others as Aaron's rod swallowed up the rods of Pharaoh's wizards"
("The Swaying Form: A Problem in Poetry"). How enviably the
poems of Howard Nemerov provide us unique names for light and
season, for mutability, reminiscence, and sympathy, to list a handful
—all conspiring ultimately to mint the new terms for our undeni-
able states of mind. Those who are reading Nemerov in any depth for
the first time will find themselves saying often, "Yes. That is right."

Those who have known him all this while will, no doubt, remember having said the same thing many times before about his poems.

If Nemerov is learned and professorial on the page, he is also irreverent, droll, and compassionate. He reminds us that thoughtfulness is the secret of all poems, and that our original poets were, in his own words, "the first great listeners, attuned / To interval, relationship and scale[.]" Perhaps most importantly, he is a writer who offers us a model of what it means to think and see poetically. What is literature, after all, if not a vehicle to understanding, a lens through which we view the momentary replications of our lives? Howard Nemerov was a master of moments, and he somehow knew, as did Frost and Yeats and Keats, the way to make them our moments as well. It demands, in the end, a kind of selflessness that he consistently exhibited. It demands, too, an understanding that it is not the artist but the art (and all the powers of thought and imagination contained therein) that matters most. "[P]oems are not / The point[,]" as Nemerov writes in "The Blue Swallows":

. . . Finding again the world,
That is the point, where loveliness
Adorns intelligible things
Because the mind's eye lit the sun.

Daniel Anderson

Acknowledgments

I would like to express my gratitude to Margaret Nemerov for her cooperation on this book. I would also like to thank Randolph Petilos and Perry Cartwright at the University of Chicago Press for their encouragement and practical assistance. Bill Baer, editor of *The Formalist*, was kind enough to send me the issue of his magazine (vol. 12, no. 1, 2001) devoted entirely to Howard Nemerov; complete with poetry, criticism, an interview, and selected remembrances, it is a touching and graceful tribute to the poet. The excitement and alacrity with which David Sanders at Ohio University Press accepted the proposal for this collection was, to say the least, inspirational. I have enjoyed his good humor and insightful conversation. Thanks, finally, to John Grammer, Andrew Hudgins, and Wyatt Prunty— good friends and benevolent tutors.

D.A.

FROM

The Image and the Law

1947

The Truth of the Matter

The Sunday papers are on the streets.
Several people starved in Bucharest.
Read (because the truth is black and white)
The truth. When one reads it is
As much the black as the white that
One reads, construing the letters.

Here the human faces are gray as
Old bread, where the camera has
Stopped two or three on a gray day
In a sky that seems to be raining.
Words show that these faces have shuddered
Instantaneously from, say, Madrid.

The citizen reads the Sunday papers.
He thanks his God he is not
In Posnan or Allenstein or Belgrade.
He is, for example, in Chicago.
The world situation is terrible,
The famine a terrible thing.

The head of a great sugar refinery
Has died of diabetes. That sounds right:
The citizen considers divine justice,
Reads further of the Ministers at Paris:
A person with a flaming sword has been
Arrested in the rain, in Schenectady.

On Monday morning the truth comes
In smaller packages, neat and pale
With a brand of words over the brow.
On Monday the wisdom of Sunday
Drifts on the gutter tides. The pale,
The staring faces, twirl around and go down.

Observation of October

An old desperation of the flesh.
Mortification and revivification
Of the spirit. There are those
Who work outdoors, and others
Who pull down blinds against the sun.

A cold October day I find
Fear of death in the weather, for
Those in the streets are hurrying,
And those at home take hot baths
Or pace the floor and refuse to go out.

And many, winter approaching,
Go early to bed at night, refuse
To admit their friends or read the papers,
And sleep curled up. There are, I think,
Simplicities in every life.

The Fortune Teller

The fortune teller, certainly a fake,
Quite rightly holds you in contempt, for she
(Though she take your hand before she speak,
Nor can you question her sincerity)
Suspects the wisdom of your lucky break:
She knows the dark man and the ocean passage
For envoys of uncertain embassage
That may be evil (but their fortunes rise)
Or may be good, until they equalize.

She understands the fate you seek must bear
What fate's already given, or will give;
And views you with an intimate despair
That chuckles mournfully, but cannot grieve.
She prophesies, without asking to share,
Portals to fortune that can swing both ways
And boodle independent of your essays.
When you have gone she may, remotely, weep
At vague ambitions quartered on her sleep:

But not for you, whom she has sent away
With fortune of a sort, sentenced to wait,
Piously turning corners every day,
Computing and interpreting your fate:
Regretting departure but afraid to stay.
She cries, quietly in her mind, for reason
Unwise as that you cry for, under question
In constant session of another's lust,
Which she may bear some after you are dust.

FROM

Guide to the Ruins

1950

Guide to the Ruins

One lives by commerce, said the guide.
One sells the available thing, time
And again: the ruins, the temple grove,
The gods with their noses knocked off.
One profits by the view.

It is a difficult trade, he said,
To give to the dishonored dead
Their stature and their stony eyes.
The vulgar paint has flaked away
Leaving the color of time,

The unimpassioned grey which is
Not now in commodious demand.
One gives, with broken Herakles,
A premium of legend, a pamphlet
To certify the chill.

What is it that one sells, the self?
I think not. One sells always time
Dissembled in heroic stone: such eyes
As look like cloud-reflecting lakes
In the old mountains of time.

Elegy of Last Resort

The boardwalks are empty, the cafés closed,
The bathchairs in mute squadrons face the sea.
Grey cloud goes over, the baffled involved brain
Of the old god over the vacant waters:
The proprietors of the world have gone home.

The girls, the senators, the priests, are gone,
Whose gowns the summer wind billowed no less
Than this of autumn does the scarecrow's coat;
And are not otherwise remembered than
As ideas of death in the dry sand blowing.

Aschenbach is dead, and other invalids
Have coughed their poems and died in bed.
The sea wind salts the rotting timbers,
Sand rattles against the empty windows,
Last week's newspapers crumple at the wall.

These visitors of smoke in sallow light
Curl, drift, dissolve to seaward in the wind.
They were the piteous shapes of accident
Whose winter substance ate and drank elsewhere
Time's rigors: a harder bread, more acid wine.

And some doubtless with sullen breath do praise
Autumnal pieties: the speech against
Nothing, and meaning nothing; the pain of prayer
That time's corrupted body will not hear;
The unfriendly marriage in the stranger's house.

We enter again November, and the last
Steep fall of time into the deep of time,
Atlantic and defeated, and to die
In the perplexity of a sour world
Whose mighty dispensations all are done.

This shoulder of the earth turns from the sun
Into the great darkness, into the steep
Valley of the stars, into the pit
Of frozen Cocytus, where Satan stands
Wielding the world upon his pain and pride.

We enter again November: cold late light
Glazes the field. A little fever of love,
Held in numbed hands, admires the false gods;
While lonely on this coast the sea bids us
Farewell, and the salt crust hardens toward winter.

The Salt Garden

1955

The Winter Lightning

for Paul

Over the snow at night,
And while the snow still fell,
A sky torn to the bone
Shattered the ghostly world with light;
As though this were the moon's hell,
A world hard as a stone,
    Cold, and blue-white.

As if the storming sea
Should sunder to its floor,
And all things hidden there
Gleam in the moment silently,
So does the meadow at the door
To split and sudden air
    Show stone and tree.

From the drowned world of dark
The sleeping innocence
Surrenders all its seeming;
Under the high, charged carbon arc
Light of the world, a guilty sense
Stiffens the secret dreaming
    Animal park.

So in the camera's glare
The fortunate and famed,
For all their crooked smiles,
Reveal through their regarded stare

How all that's publicly acclaimed
One brutal flash reviles
    For cold despair.

So is the murderer caught
When his lost victim rises
Glaring through dream and light
With icy eyes. That which was thought
In secret, and after wore disguises,
Silts up the drowning sight
    Mind inwrought.

So may the poem dispart
The mirror from the light
Where none can see a seam;
The poet, from his wintry heart
And in the lightning second's sight,
Illuminate this dream
    With a cold art.

Zalmoxis

The way spring comes this time, with a soft
Suddenness: after the robin-snow a rain,
After the rain the sun in a ragged cloud
Making a mild mist on the cold meadows,
On stone walls veined with ice, on blind windows
Burnt red beneath the southward slate of houses.

From the pale, yellow and peeled branches of willow
And alder the globes of water grow and fall
In ripenings of light; and a crystal thread,
Enlaced with the needles of the pine, silvers
The earliest sketches of the spider, softens
Coldly to life the leaves of pupal sleep.

Warm in the house, at the bright window's edge,
A fly crawls on the dry, leathery spines
Of the sleeping dramatists; the speckled dust,
In the long light's line between the blinds,
Dances until the scholar's ancient eye
Lights between sleep and waking. He leaves his book,

And, rising, he throws open the window wide,
Watches cigar smoke swaying in the room
Till smoke and dream dissolve in air together;
Then stares down the field to the wild hill,
Where on this day the sullen and powerful bear,
Drunken with deathlessness, lurches from sleep.

The Pond

At the long meadow's end, where the road runs
High on a bank, making a kind of wall,
The rains of last October slowly built
Us up this pond some hundred yards across
And deep maybe to the height of a man's thigh
At the deepest place. It was surprising how
Slowly the water gained across the land
All autumn, no one noticing, until
We had the pond where none had been before
To any memory—most surprising in
This country where we think of contours as
Fixed on a map and named and permanent,
Where even if a stream runs dry in summer
You have the stream-bed still to go by and
The chartered name—Red Branch, and Henry's Creek,
And Anthony's Race—for reassurance, though
The reason of those names be sunken with
The men who named them so, in the natural past
Before our history began to be
Written in book or map; our history,
Or the settled story that we give the world
Out of the mouths of crones and poachers
Remembering or making up our kinship
In the overgrown swamplands of the mind;
And precious little reassurance, if
You think of it, but enough about that.
Here was, at any rate, surprisingly,
This piece of water covering the ground:
Clear blue, and pale, and crisping up to black
Squalls when the north wind moved across its face;

The question whether it would go or stay
Never came up, and no one gave it a name—
Only the water-birds on their way south
Accepted it, and rested there at night,
Coming at dusk down the meadow on wide wings
And splashing up on beating wings at dawn.

By Christmastime the pond was frozen solid
Under a foot of snow, level and white
Across the meadow so you couldn't say
Except from memory where the water was
And where the land; and maybe no grown-up
Would have remembered, but the children did
And brought their skates, and someone's father patched
Together a plough from plank and two-by-four
That half-a-dozen kids could lean against
And clear the snow down to the glittering ice.
They skated all the darkening afternoons
Until the sun burnt level on the ice,
And built their fires all along the shore
To warm their hands and feet, and skated nights
Under the full moon or the dark; the ice
Mirrored the moon's light, or the fire's, cold.
There was a tragedy, if that is what
One calls it, the newspapers called it that:
"Pond Claims First Victim" (it still had no name),
As though a monster underneath the ice
Had been in wait to capture the little boy
Skating in darkness all alone, away
From the firelight—the others heard his cry
But he was gone before they found the place—,
Or else as though, a tribe of savages,
We sanctified our sports with sacrifice.

At any rate, the skating didn't stop
Despite the funeral and motherly gloom
And editorials; what happened was
The pond took the boy's name of Christopher,
And this was voted properly in meeting
For a memorial and would be so
On the next map, when the next map was drawn:
Christopher Pond: if the pond should still be there.

The winter set its teeth; near Eastertide
Before the pond was free of ice all night;
And by that time the birds were coming back
Leisurely, staying a day or so before
They rose and vanished in the northward sky;
Their lonely cries across the open water
Played on the cold, sweet virginal of spring
A chaste, beginning tune carried along
With a wind out of the east. Killdeer and plover
Came and were gone; grackle, starling and flicker
Settled to stay; and the sparrowhawk would stand
In the height of noon, a stillness on beating wings,
While close over the water swallows would trace
A music nearly visible in air,
Snapping at newborn flies. Slowly the pond
Warmed into life: cocoon and bud and egg,
All winter's seed and shroud, unfolded being
In the pond named for Christopher, who drowned.
By day the birds, and then the frogs at night,
Kept up a music there, part requiem,
Part hunting-song; among the growing reeds
The water boatman worked his oar, the strider
Walked between air and water, dragonfly
Climbed to be born, and dazzled on clear wings.

Then day by day, in the heat of June, the green
World raised itself to natural arrogance,
And the air sang with summer soon to come.

In sullen August, under the massy heat
Of the sun towering in the height, I sat
At the pond's edge, the indeterminate
Soft border of what no longer was a pond
But a swamp, a marsh, with here and there a stretch
Of open water, even that half spread
With lily pads and the rich flesh of lilies.
And elsewhere life was choking on itself
As though, in spite of all the feeding there,
Death could not keep the pace and had to let
Life curb itself: pondweed and pickerel-weed
And bladderwort, eel-grass and delicate
Sundew and milfoil, peopled thick the city
Of themselves; and dragonfly and damselfly
By hundreds darted among the clustering leaves,
Striders by hundreds skated among the stalks
Of pitcher-plant and catkin; breathless the air
Under the intense quiet whining of
All things striving to breathe; the gift of life
Turning its inward heat upon itself.
So, Christopher, I thought, this is the end
Of dedication, and of the small death
We sought to make a name and sacrifice.
The long year has turned away, and the pond
Is drying up, while its remaining life
Grasps at its own throat: the proud lilies wilt,
The milfoil withers, catkins crack and fall,
The dragonfly glitters over it all;
All that your body and your given name

Could do in accidental consecrations
Against nature, returns to nature now,
And so, Christopher, goodbye.
                              But with these thoughts
There came a dragonfly and settled down
On a stem before my eyes, and made me think
How in nature too there is a history,
And that this winged animal of light,
Before it could delight the eye, had been
In a small way a dragon of the deep,
A killer and meat-eater on the floor
Beneath the April surface of the pond;
And that it rose and cast its kind in May
As though putting away costume and mask
In the bitter play, and taking a lighter part.
And thinking so, I saw with a new eye
How nothing given us to keep is lost
Till we are lost, and immortality
Is ours until we have no use for it
And live anonymous in nature's name
Though named in human memory and art.
Not consolation, Christopher, though rain
Fill up the pond again and keep your name
Bright as the glittering water in the spring;
Not consolation, but our acquiescence.
And I made this song for a memorial
Of yourself, boy, and the dragonfly together.

The Goose Fish

On the long shore, lit by the moon
To show them properly alone,
Two lovers suddenly embraced
So that their shadows were as one.
The ordinary night was graced
For them by the swift tide of blood
That silently they took at flood,
And for a little time they prized
    Themselves emparadised.

Then, as if shaken by stage-fright
Beneath the hard moon's bony light,
They stood together on the sand
Embarrassed in each other's sight
But still conspiring hand in hand,
Until they saw, there underfoot,
As though the world had found them out,
The goose fish turning up, though dead,
    His hugely grinning head.

There in the china light he lay,
Most ancient and corrupt and grey.
They hesitated at his smile,
Wondering what it seemed to say
To lovers who a little while
Before had thought to understand,
By violence upon the sand,

The only way that could be known
   To make a world their own.

It was a wide and moony grin
Together peaceful and obscene;
They knew not what he would express,
So finished a comedian
He might mean failure or success,
But took it for an emblem of
Their sudden, new and guilty love
To be observed by, when they kissed,
   That rigid optimist.

So he became their patriarch,
Dreadfully mild in the half-dark.
His throat that the sand seemed to choke,
His picket teeth, these left their mark
But never did explain the joke
That so amused him, lying there
While the moon went down to disappear
Along the still and tilted track
   That bears the zodiac.

The Snow Globe

A long time ago, when I was a child,
They left my light on while I went to sleep,
As though they would have wanted me beguiled
By brightness if at all; dark was too deep.

And they left me one toy, a village white
With the fresh snow and silently in glass
Frozen forever. But if you shook it,
The snow would rise up in the rounded space

And from the limits of the universe
Snow itself down again. O world of white,
First home of dreams! Now that I have my dead,
I want so cold an emblem to rehearse
How many of them have gone from the world's light,
As I have gone, too, from my snowy bed.

Central Park

The broad field darkens, but, still moving round
So that they seem to hover off the ground,
Children are following a shadowy ball;
Shrill, as of birds, their high voices sound.

The pale December sky at darkfall seems
A lake of ice, and frozen there the gleams
Of the gaunt street-lamps and the young cold cries,
The ball falling in the slow distance of dreams.

Football, long falling in the winter sky,
The cold climate of a child's eye
Had kept you at the height so long a time;
His ear had kept the waiting player's cry,

That after years, coming that way then,
He might be pity's witness among men
Who hear those cries across the darkening field,
And see the shadow children home again.

The Market-Place

Do you know me, my lord?
Excellent well; you are a fishmonger.

The armored salmon jewel the ice with blood
Where cobblestones are steaming in the sun.
Witness my heart drains deep, if now, at noon,
Soft August of the salt corrupting year
Stirs a chill cloud, raises a silver flood
To savage in the marrow of my weir.

FROM

Mirrors and Windows

1958

The Mirror

O room of silences, alien land
Where likeness lies, how should I understand
What happens here as in the other world
But silently, the branch, the same leaf curled
Against the branch, stirred in the same breeze,
And all those quivering duplicities
Rendered again under a distant light?

Now slowly the snow drifts down, and coming night
Darkens the room, while in the leaden glass
I watch with observed eyes the stranger pass.

Trees

To be a giant and keep quiet about it,
To stay in one's own place;
To stand for the constant presence of process
And always to seem the same;
To be steady as a rock and always trembling,
Having the hard appearance of death
With the soft, fluent nature of growth,
One's Being deceptively armored,
One's Becoming deceptively vulnerable;
To be so tough, and take the light so well,
Freely providing forbidden knowledge
Of so many things about heaven and earth
For which we should otherwise have no word—
Poems or people are rarely so lovely,
And even when they have great qualities
They tend to tell you rather than exemplify
What they believe themselves to be about,
While from the moving silence of trees,
Whether in storm or calm, in leaf and naked,
Night or day, we draw conclusions of our own,
Sustaining and unnoticed as our breath,
And perilous also—though there has never been
A critical tree—about the nature of things.

The Town Dump

"The art of our necessities is strange,
That can make vile things precious."

A mile out in the marshes, under a sky
Which seems to be always going away
In a hurry, on that Venetian land threaded
With hidden canals, you will find the city
Which seconds ours (so cemeteries, too,
Reflect a town from hillsides out of town),
Where Being most Becomingly ends up
Becoming some more. From cardboard tenements,
Windowed with cellophane, or simply tenting
In paper bags, the angry mackerel eyes
Glare at you out of stove-in, sunken heads
Far from the sea; the lobster, also, lifts
An empty claw in his most minatory
Of gestures; oyster, crab, and mussel shells
Lie here in heaps, savage as money hurled
Away at the gate of hell. If you want results,
These are results.
                    Objects of value or virtue,
However, are also to be picked up here,
Though rarely, lying with bones and rotten meat,
Eggshells and mouldy bread, banana peels
No one will skid on, apple cores that caused
Neither the fall of man nor a theory
Of gravitation. People do throw out
The family pearls by accident, sometimes,
Not often; I've known dealers in antiques
To prowl this place by night, with flashlights, on

The off-chance of somebody's having left
Derelict chairs which will turn out to be
By Hepplewhite, a perfect set of six
Going to show, I guess, that in any sty
Someone's heaven may open and shower down
Riches responsive to the right dream; though
It is a small chance, certainly, that sends
The ghostly dealer, heavy with fly-netting
Over his head, across these hills in darkness,
Stumbling in cut-glass goblets, lacquered cups,
And other products of his dreamy midden
Penciled with light and guarded by the flies.

For there are flies, of course. A dynamo
Composed, by thousands, of our ancient black
Retainers, hums here day and night, steady
As someone telling beads, the hum becoming
A high whine at any disturbance; then,
Settled again, they shine under the sun
Like oil-drops, or are invisible as night,
By night.
        All this continually smoulders,
Crackles, and smokes with mostly invisible fires
Which, working deep, rarely flash out and flare,
And never finish. Nothing finishes;
The flies, feeling the heat, keep on the move.

Among the flies, the purefying fires,
The hunters by night, acquainted with the art
Of our necessities, and the new deposits
That each day wastes with treasure, you may say
There should be ratios. You may sum up

The results, if you want results. But I will add
That wild birds, drawn to the carrion and flies,
Assemble in some numbers here, their wings
Shining with light, their flight enviably free,
Their music marvelous, though sad, and strange.

Storm Windows

People are putting up storm windows now,
Or were, this morning, until the heavy rain
Drove them indoors. So, coming home at noon,
I saw storm windows lying on the ground,
Frame-full of rain; through the water and glass
I saw the crushed grass, how it seemed to stream
Away in lines like seaweed on the tide
Or blades of wheat leaning under the wind.
The ripple and splash of rain on the blurred glass
Seemed that it briefly said, as I walked by,
Something I should have liked to say to you,
Something . . . the dry grass bent under the pane
Brimful of bouncing water . . . something of
A swaying clarity which blindly echoes
This lonely afternoon of memories
And missed desires, while the wintry rain
(Unspeakable, the distance in the mind!)
Runs on the standing windows and away.

Shells

You pick one up along the shore.
It is empty and light and dry,
And leaves a powdery chalk on your hands.

The life that made it is gone out.
That is what is meant when people say,
"A hollow shell," "a shell of his former self,"

Failing to take into account
The vital waste in composition
With the beauty of the ruined remainder

Which is no use to anyone,
Of course, unless as decoration:
A Souvenir of Sunset Beach, etc.

Its form is only cryptically
Instructive, if at all: it winds
Like generality, from nothing to nothing

By means of nothing but itself.
It is a stairway going nowhere,
Our precious emblem of the steep ascent,

Perhaps, beginning at a point
And opening to infinity,
Or the other way, if you want it the other way.

Inside it, also, there is nothing
Except the obedient sound of waters
Beat by your Mediterranean, classic heart

In bloody tides as long as breath,
Bringing by turns the ebb and flood
Upon the ruining house of histories,

Whose whitening stones, in Africa,
Bake dry and blow away, in Athens,
In Rome, abstract and instructive as chalk

When children scrawl the blackboard full
Of wild spirals every which way,
To be erased with chalk dust, then with water.

The Statues in the Public Gardens

Alone at the end of green *allées*, alone
Where a path turns back upon itself, or else
Where several paths converge, green bronze, grey stone,
The weatherbeaten famous figures wait
Inside their basins, on their pedestals,
Till time, as promised them, wears out of date.

Around them rise the willow, birch, and elm,
Sweet shaken pliancies in the weather now.
The granite hand is steady on the helm,
The sword, the pen, unshaken in the hand,
The bandage and the laurel on the brow:
The last obedience is the last command.

Children and nurses eddying through the day,
Old gentlemen with newspapers and canes,
And licit lovers, public as a play,
Never acknowledge the high regard of fame
Across their heads—the patriot's glare, the pains
Of prose—and scarcely stop to read a name.

Children, to be illustrious is sad.
Do not look up. Those empty eyes are stars,
Their glance the constellation of the mad
Who must be turned to stone. To save your garden,
My playful ones, these pallid voyagers
Stand in the streak of rain, imploring pardon.

At night the other lovers come to play
Endangered games, and robbers lie in wait

To knock old ladies with a rock; but they
Tremble to come upon these stony men
And suffragettes, who shine like final fate
In the electric green of every glen.

For it is then that statues suffer their
Sacrificed lives, and sigh through fruitless trees
After the flesh. Their sighs tremble the air,
They would surrender scepters, swords, and globes,
Feeling the soft flank shudder to the breeze
Under the greatcoats and the noble robes.

In darker glades, the nearly naked stone
Of athlete, goddess chaste as any snows
That stain them winters, tempts maiden and man
From their prosthetic immortality:
Pythagoras' thigh, or Tycho's golden nose,
For a figleaf fallen from the withered tree.

A Day on the Big Branch

Still half drunk, after a night at cards,
with the grey dawn taking us unaware
among our guilty kings and queens, we drove
far North in the morning, winners, losers,
to a stream in the high hills, to climb up to a place
one of us knew, with some vague view
of cutting losses or consolidating gains
by the old standard appeal to the wilderness,
the desert, the empty places of our exile,
bringing only the biblical bread and cheese
and cigarettes got from a grocer's on the way,
expecting to drink only the clear cold water
among the stones, and remember, or forget.
Though no one said anything about atonement,
there was still some purgatorial idea
in all those aching heads and ageing hearts
as we climbed the giant stair of the stream,
reaching the place around noon.

It was as promised, a wonder, with granite walls
enclosing ledges, long and flat, of limestone,
or, rolling, of lava; within the ledges
the water, fast and still, pouring its yellow light,
and green, over the tilted slabs of the floor,
blackened at shady corners, falling in a foam
of crystal to a calm where the waterlight
dappled the ledges as they leaned
against the sun; big blue dragonflies hovered
and darted and dipped a wing, hovered again

against the low wind moving over the stream,
and shook the flakes of light from their clear wings.
This surely was it, was what we had come for,
was nature, though it looked like art with its
grey fortress walls and laminated benches
as in the waiting room of some petrified station.
But we believed; and what it was we believed
made of the place a paradise
for ruined poker players, win or lose,
who stripped naked and bathed and dried out on the rocks
like gasping trout (the water they drank
making them drunk again), lit cigarettes and lay back
waiting for nature to say the last word
—as though the stones were Memnon stones,
which, caught in a certain light, would sing.

The silence (and even the noise of the waters
was silence) grew pregnant; that is the phrase,
grew pregnant; but nothing else did.
The mountain brought forth not a mouse, and the rocks,
unlike the ones you would expect to find
on the slopes of Purgatory or near Helicon,
mollified by muses and with a little give to 'em,
were modern American rocks, and hard as rocks.
Our easy bones groaned, our flesh baked
on one side and shuddered on the other; and each man
thought bitterly about primitive simplicity
and decadence, and how he had been ruined
by civilization and forced by circumstances
to drink and smoke and sit up all night
inspecting those perfectly arbitrary cards
until he was broken-winded as a trout on a rock
and had no use for the doctrines of Jean Jacques

Rousseau, and could no longer afford
a savagery whether noble or not; some
would never batter that battered copy of Walden
again.

But all the same,
the water, the sunlight, and the wind
did something; even the dragonflies
did something to the minds full of telephone
numbers and flushes, to the flesh
sweating bourbon on one side and freezing on the other.
And the rocks, the old and tumbling boulders
which formed the giant stair of the stream,
induced (again) some purgatorial ideas
concerning humility, concerning patience
and enduring what had to be endured,
winning and losing and breaking even;
ideas of weathering in whatever weather,
being eroded, or broken, or ground down into pebbles
by the stream's necessitous and grave currents.
But to these ideas did any purgatory
respond? Only this one: that in a world
where even the Memnon stones were carved in soap
one might at any rate wash with the soap.

After a time we talked about the War,
about what we had done in the War, and how near
some of us had been to being drowned, and burned,
and shot, and how many people we knew
who had been drowned, or burned, or shot;
and would it have been better to have died
in the War, the peaceful old War, where we were young?
But the mineral peace, or paralysis, of those

great stones, the moving stillness of the waters,
entered our speech; the ribs and blood
of the earth, from which all fables grow,
established poetry and truth in us,
so that at last one said, "I shall play cards
until the day I die," and another said,
"in bourbon whisky are all the vitamins
and minerals needed to sustain man's life,"
and still another, "I shall live on smoke
until my spirit has been cured of flesh."

Climbing downstream again, on the way home
to the lives we had left empty for a day,
we noticed, as not before, how of three bridges
not one had held the stream, which in its floods
had twisted the girders, splintered the boards, hurled
boulder on boulder, and had broken into rubble,
smashed practically back to nature,
the massive masonry of span after span
with its indifferent rage; this was a sight
that sobered us considerably, and kept us quiet
both during the long drive home and after,
till it was time to deal the cards.

The Loon's Cry

On a cold evening, summer almost gone,
I walked alone down where the railroad bridge
Divides the river from the estuary.
There was a silence over both the waters,
The river's concentrated reach, the wide
Diffusion of the delta, marsh and sea,
Which in the distance misted out of sight.

As on the seaward side the sun went down,
The river answered with the rising moon,
Full moon, its craters, mountains and still seas
Shining like snow and shadows on the snow.
The balanced silence centered where I stood,
The fulcrum of two poised immensities,
Which offered to be weighed at either hand.

But I could think only, Red sun, white moon,
This is a natural beauty, it is not
Theology. For I had fallen from
The symboled world, where I in earlier days
Found mysteries of meaning, form, and fate
Signed on the sky, and now stood but between
A swamp of fire and a reflecting rock.

I envied those past ages of the world
When, as I thought, the energy in things
Shone through their shapes, when sun and moon no less
Than tree or stone or star or human face
Were seen but as fantastic Japanese

Lanterns are seen, sullen or gay colors
And lines revealing the light that they conceal.

The world a stage, its people maskers all
In actions largely framed to imitate
God and His Lucifer's long debate, a trunk
From which, complex and clear, the episodes
Spread out their branches. Each life played a part,
And every part consumed a life, nor dreams
After remained to mock accomplishment.

Under the austere power of the scene,
The moon standing balanced against the sun,
I simplified still more, and thought that now
We'd traded all those mysteries in for things,
For essences in things, not understood—
Reality in things! and now we saw
Reality exhausted all their truth.

As answering my thought a loon cried out
Laughter of desolation on the river,
A savage cry, now that the moon went up
And the sun down—yet when I heard him cry
Again, his voice seemed emptied of that sense
Or any other, and Adam I became,
Hearing the first loon cry in paradise.

For sometimes, when the world is not our home
Nor have we any home elsewhere, but all
Things look to leave us naked, hungry, cold,
We suddenly may seem in paradise
Again, in ignorance and emptiness

Blessed beyond all that we thought to know:
Then on sweet waters echoes the loon's cry.

I thought I understood what that cry meant,
That its contempt was for the forms of things,
Their doctrines, which decayed—the nouns of stone
And adjectives of glass—not for the verb
Which surged in power properly eternal
Against the seawall of the solid world,
Battering and undermining what it built,

And whose respeaking was the poet's act,
Only and always, in whatever time
Stripped by uncertainty, despair, and ruin,
Time readying to die, unable to die
But damned to life again, and the loon's cry.
And now the sun was sunken in the sea,
The full moon high, and stars began to shine.

The moon, I thought, might have been such a world
As this one is, till it went cold inside,
Nor any strength of sun could keep its people
Warm in their palaces of glass and stone.
Now all its craters, mountains and still seas,
Shining like snow and shadows on the snow,
Orbit this world in envy and late love.

And the stars too? Worlds, as the scholars taught
So long ago? Chaos of beauty, void,
O burning cold, against which we define
Both wretchedness and love. For signatures
In all things are, which leave us not alone

Even in the thought of death, and may by arts
Contemplative be found and named again.

The loon again? Or else a whistling train,
Whose far thunders began to shake the bridge.
And it came on, a loud bulk under smoke,
Changing the signals on the bridge, the bright
Rubies and emeralds, rubies and emeralds
Signing the cold night as I turned for home,
Hearing the train cry once more, like a loon.

A Primer of the Daily Round

A peels an apple, while B kneels to God,
C telephones to D, who has a hand
On E's knee, F coughs, G turns up the sod
For H's grave, I do not understand
But J is bringing one clay pigeon down
While K brings down a nightstick on L's head,
And M takes mustard, N drives into town,
O goes to bed with P, and Q drops dead,
R lies to S, but happens to be heard
By T, who tells U not to fire V
For having to give W the word
That X is now deceiving Y with Z,
    Who happens just now to remember A
    Peeling an apple somewhere far away.

Brainstorm

The house was shaken by a rising wind
That rattled window and door. He sat alone
In an upstairs room and heard these things: a blind
Ran up with a bang, a door slammed, a groan
Came from some hidden joist, and a leaky tap,
At any silence of the wind, walked like
A blind man through the house. Timber and sap
Revolt, he thought, from washer, baulk and spike.
Bent to his book, continued unafraid
Until the crows came down from their loud flight
To walk along the rooftree overhead.
Their horny feet, so near but out of sight,
Scratched on the slate; when they were blown away
He heard their wings beat till they came again,
While the wind rose, and the house seemed to sway,
And window panes began to blind with rain.
The house was talking, not to him, he thought,
But to the crows; the crows were talking back
In their black voices. The secret might be out:
Houses are only trees stretched on the rack.
And once the crows knew, all nature would know.
Fur, leaf and feather would invade the form,
Nail rust with rain and shingle warp with snow,
Vine tear the wall, till any straw-borne storm
Could rip both roof and rooftree off and show
Naked to nature what they had kept warm.

He came to feel the crows walk on his head
As if he were the house, their crooked feet

Scratched, through the hair, his scalp. He might be dead
It seemed, and all the noises underneath
Be but the cooling of the sinews, veins,
Juices, and sodden sacks suddenly let go;
While in his ruins of wiring, his burst mains,
The rainy wind had been set free to blow
Until the green uprising and mob rule
That ran the world had taken over him,
Split him like seed, and set him in the school
Where any crutch can learn to be a limb.

Inside his head he heard the stormy crows.

Painting a Mountain Stream

Running and standing still at once
is the whole truth. Raveled or combed,
wrinkled or clear, it gets its force
from losing force. Going it stays.

Pulse beats, and planets echo this,
the running down, the standing still,
all thunder of the one thought.
The mind that thinks it is unfounded.

I speak of what is running down.
Of sun, of thunder bearing the rain
I do not speak, of the rising flame
or the slow towering of the elm.

A comb was found in a girl's grave
(ah heartsblood raveled like a rope).
The visible way is always down
but there is no floor to the world.

Study this rhythm, not this thing.
The brush's tip streams from the wrist
of a living man, a dying man.
The running water is the wrist.

In the confluence of the wrist
things and ideas ripple together,
as in the clear lake of the eye,
unfathomably, running remains.

The eye travels on running water,
out to the sky, if you let it go.
However often you call it back
it travels again, out to the sky.

The water that seemed to stand is gone.
The water that seemed to run is here.
Steady the wrist, steady the eye;
paint this rhythm, not this thing.

FROM

New Poems

1960

Moment

Now, starflake frozen on the windowpane
All of a winter night, the open hearth
Blazing beyond Andromeda, the sea-
Anemone and the downwind seed, O moment
Hastening, halting in a clockwise dust,
The time in all the hospitals is now,
Under the arc-lights where the sentry walks
His lonely wall it never moves from now,
The crying in the cell is also now,
And now is quiet in the tomb as now
Explodes inside the sun, and it is now
In the saddle of space, where argosies of dust
Sail outward blazing, and the mind of God,
The flash across the gap of being, thinks
In the instant absence of forever: now.

Runes

" . . . *insaniebam salubriter et moriebar vitaliter.*"

St. Augustine

I

This is about the stillness in moving things,
In running water, also in the sleep
Of winter seeds, where time to come has tensed
Itself, enciphering a script so fine
Only the hourglass can magnify it, only
The years unfold its sentence from the root.
I have considered such things often, but
I cannot say I have thought deeply of them:
That is my theme, of thought and the defeat
Of thought before its object, where it turns
As from a mirror, and returns to be
The thought of something and the thought of thought,
A trader doubly burdened, commercing
Out of one stillness and into another.

II

About Ulysses, the learned have reached two
Distinct conclusions. In one, he secretly
Returns to Ithaca, is recognized
By Euryclea, destroys the insolent suitors,
And makes himself known to Penelope,
Describing the bed he built; then, at the last

Dissolve, we see him with Telemachus
Leaving the palace, planning to steal sheep:
The country squire resumes a normal life.
But in the other, out beyond the gates
Of Hercules, gabbling persuasively
About virtue and knowledge, he sails south
To disappear from sight behind the sun;
Drowning near blessed shores he flames in hell.
I do not know which ending is the right one.

III

Sunflowers, traders rounding the horn of time
Into deep afternoons, sleepy with gain,
The fall of silence has begun to storm
Around you where you nod your heavy heads
Whose bare poles, raking out of true, will crack,
Driving your wreckage on the world's lee shore.
Your faces no more will follow the sun,
But bow down to the ground with a heavy truth
That dereliction learns, how charity
Is strangled out of selfishness at last;
When, golden misers in the courts of summer,
You are stripped of gain for coining images
And broken on this quarter of the wheel,
It is on savage ground you spill yourselves,
And spend the tarnished silver of your change.

IV

The seed sleeps in the furnaces of death,
A cock's egg slept till hatching by a serpent
Wound in his wintry coil, a spring so tight
In his radical presence that every tense
Is now. Out of this head the terms of kind,
Distributed in syntax, come to judgment,
Are basilisks who write our sentences
Deep at the scripture's pith, in rooted tongues,
How one shall marry while another dies.
Give us our ignorance, the family tree
Grows upside down and shakes its heavy fruit,
Whose buried stones philosophers have sought.
For each stone bears the living word, each word
Will be made flesh, and all flesh fall to seed:
Such stones from the tree; and from the stones, such blood.

V

The fat time of the year is also time
Of the Atonement; birds to the berry bushes,
Men to the harvest; a time to answer for
Both present plenty and emptiness to come.
When the slain legal deer is salted down,
When apples smell like goodness, cold in the cellar,
You hear the ram's horn sounded in the high
Mount of the Lord, and you lift up your eyes
As though by this observance you might hide
The dry husk of an eaten heart which brings
Nothing to offer up, no sacrifice

Acceptable but the canceled-out desires
And satisfactions of another year's
Abscess, whose zero in His winter's mercy
Still hides the undecipherable seed.

VI

White water now in the snowflake's prison,
A mad king in a skullcap thinks these thoughts
In regular hexagons, each one unlike
Each of the others. The atoms of memory,
Like those that Democritus knew, have hooks
At either end, but these? Insane tycoon,
These are the riches of order snowed without end
In this distracted globe, where is no state
To fingerprint the flakes or number these
Moments melting in flight, seeds mirroring
Substance without position or a speed
And course unsubstanced. What may the spring be,
Deep in the atom, among galactic snows,
But the substance of things hoped for, argument
Of things unseen? White water, fall and fall.

VII

Unstable as water, thou shalt not excel
—Said to the firstborn, the dignity and strength,
And the defiler of his father's bed.
Fit motto for a dehydrated age
Nervously watering whisky and stock,

Quick-freezing dreams into realities.
Brain-surgeons have produced the proustian syndrome,
But patients dunk their tasteless madeleines
In vain, those papers that the Japanese
Amused themselves by watering until
They flowered and became Combray, flower
No more. The plastic and cosmetic arts
Unbreakably record the last word and
The least word, till sometimes even the Muse,
In her transparent raincoat, resembles a condom.

VIII

To go low, to be as nothing, to die,
To sleep in the dark water threading through
The fields of ice, the soapy, frothing water
That slithers under the culvert below the road,
Water of dirt, water of death, dark water,
And through the tangle of the sleeping roots
Under the coppery cold beech woods, the green
Pinewoods, and past the buried hulls of things
To come, and humbly through the breathing dreams
Of all small creatures sleeping in the earth;
To fall with the weight of things down on the one
Still ebbing stream, to go on to the end
With the convict hunted through the swamp all night.
The dog's corpse in the ditch, to come at last
Into the pit where zero's eye is closed.

IX

In this dehydrated time of digests, pills
And condensations, the most expensive presents
Are thought to come in the smallest packages:
In atoms, for example. There are still
To be found, at carnivals, men who engrave
The Lord's Prayer on a grain of wheat for pennies,
But they are a dying race, unlike the men
Now fortunate, who bottle holy water
In plastic tears, and bury mustard seeds
In lucite lockets, and for safety sell
To be planted on the dashboard of your car
The statues, in durable celluloid,
Of Mary and St. Christopher, who both
With humble power in the world's floodwaters
Carried their heavy Savior and their Lord.

X

White water, white water, feather of a form
Between the stones, is the race run to stay
Or pass away? Your utterance is riddled,
Rainbowed and clear and cold, tasting of stone,
Its brilliance blinds me. But still I have seen,
White water, at the breaking of the ice,
When the high places render up the new
Children of water and their tumbling light
Laughter runs down the hills, and the small fist
Of the seed unclenches in the day's dazzle,
How happiness is helpless before your fall,

White water, and history is no more than
The shadows thrown by clouds on mountainsides,
A distant chill, when all is brought to pass
By rain and birth and rising of the dead.

XI

A holy man said to me, "Split the stick
And there is Jesus." When I split the stick
To the dark marrow and the splintery grain
I saw nothing that was not wood, nothing
That was not God, and I began to dream
How from the tree that stood between the rivers
Came Aaron's rod that crawled in front of Pharaoh,
And came the rod of Jesse flowering
In all the generations of the Kings,
And came the timbers of the second tree,
The sticks and yardarms of the holy three-
masted vessel whereon the Son of Man
Hung between thieves, and came the crown of thorns,
The lance and ladder, when was shed that blood
Streamed in the grain of Adam's tainted seed.

XII

Consider how the seed lost by a bird
Will harbor in its branches most remote
Descendants of the bird; while everywhere
And unobserved, the soft green stalks and tubes
Of water are hardening into wood, whose hide,

Gnarled, knotted, flowing, and its hidden grain,
Remember how the water is streaming still.
Now does the seed asleep, as in a dream
Where time is compacted under pressures of
Another order, crack open like stone
From whose division pours a stream, between
The raindrop and the sea, running in one
Direction, down, and gathering in its course
That bitter salt which spices us the food
We sweat for, and the blood and tears we shed.

XIII

There sailed out on the river, Conrad saw,
The dreams of men, the seeds of commonwealths,
The germs of Empire. To the ends of the earth
One many-veined bloodstream swayed the hulls
Of darkness gone, of darkness still to come,
And sent its tendrils steeping through the roots
Of wasted continents. That echoing pulse
Carried the ground swell of all sea-returns
Muttering under history, and its taste,
Saline and cold, was as a mirror of
The taste of human blood. The sailor leaned
To lick the mirror clean, the somber and
Immense mirror that Conrad saw, and saw
The other self, the sacred Cain of blood
Who would seed a commonwealth in the Land of Nod.

XIV

There is a threshold, that meniscus where
The strider walks on drowning waters, or
That tense, curved membrane of the camera's lens
Which darkness holds against the battering light
And the distracted drumming of the world's
Importunate plenty.—Now that threshold,
The water of the eye where the world walks
Delicately, is as a needle threaded
From the reel of a raveling stream, to stitch
Dissolving figures in a watered cloth,
A damask either-sided as the shroud
Of the lord of Ithaca, labored at in light,
Destroyed in darkness, while the spidery oars
Carry his keel across deep mysteries
To harbor in unfathomable mercies.

XV

To watch water, to watch running water
Is to know a secret, seeing the twisted rope
Of runnels on the hillside, the small freshets
Leaping and limping down the tilted field
In April's light, the green, grave and opaque
Swirl in the millpond where the current slides
To be combed and carded silver at the fall;
It is a secret. Or it is not to know
The secret, but to have it in your keeping,
A locked box, Bluebeard's room, the deathless thing

Which it is death to open. Knowing the secret,
Keeping the secret—herringbones of light
Ebbing on beaches, the huge artillery
Of tides—it is not knowing, it is not keeping,
But being the secret hidden from yourself.

Going Away

Now as the year turns toward its darkness
the car is packed, and time come to start
driving west. We have lived here
for many years and been more or less content;
now we are going away. That is how
things happen, and how into new places,
among other people, we shall carry
our lives with their peculiar memories
both happy and unhappy but either way
touched with the strange tonality
of what is gone but inalienable, the clear
and level light of a late afternoon
out on the terrace, looking to the mountains,
drinking with friends. Voices and laughter
lifted in still air, in a light
that seemed to paralyze time.
We have had kindness here, and some
unkindness; now we are going on.
Though we are young enough still
and militant enough to be resolved,
keeping our faces to the front, there is
a moment, after saying all farewells,
when we taste the dry and bitter dust
of everything that we have said and done
for many years, and our mouths are dumb,
and the easy tears will not do. Soon
the north wind will shake the leaves,
the leaves will fall. It may be

never again that we shall see them,
the strangers who stand on the steps,
smiling and waving, before the screen doors
of their suddenly forbidden houses.

The View from an Attic Window

for Francis and Barbara

I

Among the high-branching, leafless boughs
Above the roof-peaks of the town,
Snowflakes unnumberably come down.

I watched out of the attic window
The laced sway of family trees,
Intricate genealogies

Whose strict, reserved gentility,
Trembling, impossible to bow,
Received the appalling fall of snow.

All during Sunday afternoon,
Not storming, but befittingly,
Out of a still, grey, devout sky,

The snowflakes fell, until all shapes
Went under, and thickening, drunken lines
Cobwebbed the sleep of solemn pines,

Up in the attic, among many things
Inherited and out of style,
I cried, then fell asleep awhile,

Waking at night now, as the snow-
flakes from darkness to darkness go
Past yellow lights in the street below.

II

I cried because life is hopeless and beautiful.
And like a child I cried myself to sleep
High in the head of the house, feeling the hull
Beneath me pitch and roll among the steep
Mountains and valleys of the many years
    That brought me to tears.

Down in the cellar, furnace and washing machine,
Pump, fuse-box, water heater, work their hearts
Out at my life, which narrowly runs between
Them and this cemetery of spare parts
For discontinued men, whose hats and canes
    Are my rich remains.

And women, their portraits and wedding gowns
Stacked in the corners, brooding in wooden trunks;
And children's rattles, books about lions and clowns;
And headless, hanging dresses swayed like drunks
Whenever a living footstep shakes the floor,
    I mention no more;

But what I thought today, that made me cry,
Is this, that we live in two kinds of thing:
The powerful trees, thrusting into the sky
Their black patience, are one, and that branching
Relation teaches how we endure and grow;
    The other is the snow,

Falling in a white chaos from the sky,
As many as the sands of all the seas,
As all the men who died or who will die,

As stars in heaven, as leaves of all the trees;
As Abraham was promised of his seed;
　　Generations bleed,

Till I, high in the tower of my time
Among familiar ruins, began to cry
For accident, sickness, justice, war and crime,
Because all died, because I had to die.
The snow fell, the trees stood, the promise kept,
　　And a child I slept.

The Icehouse in Summer

see Amos, 3:15

A door sunk in a hillside, with a bolt
thick as the boy's arm, and behind that door
the walls of ice, melting a blue, faint light,
an air of cedar branches, sawdust, fern:
decaying seasons keeping from decay.

A summer guest, the boy had never seen
(a servant told him of it) how the lake
froze three foot thick, how farmers came with teams,
with axe and saw, to cut great blocks of ice,
translucid, marbled, glittering in the sun,
load them on sleds and drag them up the hill
to be manhandled down the narrow path
and set in courses for the summer's keeping,
the kitchen uses and luxuriousness
of the great houses. And he heard how once
a team and driver drowned in the break of spring:
the man's cry melting from the ice that summer
frightened the sherbet-eaters off the terrace.

Dust of the cedar, lost and evergreen
among the slowly blunting water walls
where the blade edge melted and the steel saw's bite
was rounded out, and the horse and rider drowned
in the red sea's blood, I was the silly child
who dreamed that riderless cry, and saw the guests
run from a ghostly wall, so long before
the winter house fell with the summer house,
and the houses, Egypt, the great houses, had an end.

The Next Room of the Dream

1962

To Clio, Muse of History

On learning that The Etruscan Warrior in the
Metropolitan Museum of Art is proved a modern forgery

One more casualty,
One more screen memory penetrated at last
To be destroyed in the endless anamnesis
Always progressing, never arriving at a cure.
My childhood in the glare of that giant form
Corrupts with history, for I too fought in the War.

He, great male beauty
That stood for the sexual thrust of power,
His target eyes inviting the universal victim
To fatal seduction, the crested and greaved
Survivor long after shield and sword are dust,
Has now become another lie about our life.

Smash the idol, of course.
Bury the pieces deep as the interest of truth
Requires. And you may in time compose the future
Smoothly without him, though it is too late
To disinfect the past of his huge effigy
By any further imposition of your hands.

But tell us no more
Enchantments, Clio. History has given
And taken away; murders become memories,
And memories become the beautiful obligations:
As with a dream interpreted by one still sleeping,
The interpretation is only the next room of the dream.

For I remember how
We children stared, learning from him
Unspeakable things about war that weren't in the books;
And how the Museum store offered for sale
His photographic reproductions in full color
With the ancient genitals blacked out.

A Spell before Winter

After the red leaf and the gold have gone,
Brought down by the wind, then by hammering rain
Bruised and discolored, when October's flame
Goes blue to guttering in the cusp, this land
Sinks deeper into silence, darker into shade.
There is a knowledge in the look of things,
The old hills hunch before the north wind blows.

Now I can see certain simplicities
In the darkening rust and tarnish of the time,
And say over the certain simplicities,
The running water and the standing stone,
The yellow haze of the willow and the black
Smoke of the elm, the silver, silent light
Where suddenly, readying toward nightfall,
The sumac's candelabrum darkly flames.
And I speak to you now with the land's voice,
It is the cold, wild land that says to you
A knowledge glimmers in the sleep of things:
The old hills hunch before the north wind blows.

Goldfish

The bearded goldfish move about the bowl
Waving disheveled rags of elegant fin
Languidly in the light; their mandarin
Manner of life, weary and cynical,

Rebukes the round world that has kept them in
Glass bubbles with a mythological
Decor of Rhineland castles on a shoal
Of pebbles pink and green. Like light in gin,

Viscous as ice first forming on a stream,
Their refined feathers fan them on to no
Remarkable purpose; they close their eyes
As, mouths reopening in new surprise
About their long imprisonment in O,
They cruise the ocean of an alien dream.

Blue Suburban

Out in the elegy country, summer evenings,
It used to be always six o'clock, or seven,
Where the fountain of the willow always wept
Over the lawn, where the shadows crept longer
But came no closer, where the talk was brilliant,
The laughter friendly, where they all were young
And taken by the darkness in surprise
That night should come and the small lights go on
In the lonely house down in the elegy country,
Where the bitter things were said and the drunken friends
Steadied themselves away in their courses
For industrious ruin or casual disaster
Under a handful of pale, permanent stars.

Burning the Leaves

This was the first day that the leaves
Came down in hordes, in hosts, a great wealth
Gambled away over the green lawn
Belonging to the house, old fry and spawn
Of the rich year converted into filth
In the beds by the walls, the gutters under the eaves.
We thought of all the generations gone
Like that, flyers, migrants, fugitives.

We come like croupiers with rakes,
To a bamboo clatter drag these winnings in,
Our windfall, firstfruits, tithes and early dead
Fallen on our holdings from overhead,
And taxable to trees against our sin.
Money to burn! We play for higher stakes
Than the mere leaves, and, burdened with treasure, tread
The orbit of the tree that heaven shakes.

The wrath of God we gather up today,
But not for long. In the beginning night
We light our hoarded leaves, the flames arise,
The smell of smoke takes memory by surprise,
And we become as children in our sight.
That is, I think, the object of this play,
Though our children dance about the sacrifice
Unthinking, their shadows lengthened and cast away.

Elegy for a Nature Poet

It was in October, a favorite season,
He went for his last walk. The covered bridge,
Most natural of all the works of reason,
Received him, let him go. Along the hedge

He rattled his stick; observed the blackening bushes
In his familiar field; thought he espied
Late meadow larks; considered picking rushes
For a dry arrangement; returned home, and died

Of a catarrh caught in the autumn rains
And let go on uncared for. He was too rapt
In contemplation to recall that brains
Like his should not be kept too long uncapped

In the wet and cold weather. While we mourned,
We thought of his imprudence, and how Nature,
Whom he'd done so much for, had finally turned
Against her creature.

His gift was daily his delight, he peeled
The landscape back to show it was a story;
Any old bird or burning bush revealed
At his hands just another allegory.

Nothing too great, nothing too trivial
For him; from mountain range or humble vermin
He could extract the hidden parable—
If need be, crack the stone to get the sermon.

And now, poor man, he's gone. Without his name
The field reverts to wilderness again,
The rocks are silent, woods don't seem the same;
Demoralized small birds will fly insane.

Rude Nature, whom he loved to idealize
And would have wed, pretends she never heard
His voice at all, as, taken by surprise
At last, he goes to her without a word.

From the Desk of the Laureate:
For Immediate Release

Because Great Pan is dead, Astraea gone,
Because the singing has ceased upon Sion,
The Well at Helicon choked up with mud,
The Master of Songs tenders his resignation.

He cannot even do the Birthday Ode
For the Queen Mother, much less manage the
Elaborated forms of Elegy
And Epithalamion, when these fall due.

The Court will simply have to get along
As best it can on Chronicles in prose.
The Master regrets, but from this day the news
Must go uncelebrated in his song.

Although the pay was low, the hours long,
He wrote his wretched little works with love;
And if he will not have his lute restrung,
His reasons are the ones set forth above.

He has retired to the ancient horrible hotel
Where he can still afford to be a swell,
His nightly pony, a scotch whisky neat,
Brought by the servingman on squeaking feet.

FROM

The Blue Swallows

1967

Landscape with Figures

What a dream of a landscape!
Cries Mrs Persepolis, and I
Agree, my gaze follows hers
Out to the giant recumbent
Hills in their sullen haze
Brooding some brutal thought
As it were about myself &
Mrs Persepolis, who are now
Alone in a closed garden
With various flowers and bees
And a feeble fountain that drips
On a stone in a heart-shaped
Pool with a single leopard-
Like toad immobilized all
Morning at his predatory
Meditation, making me think
Mrs Persepolis not too old
With her bright voice and
Wrinkling skin at the wrist
Patterned in sunburnt diamonds
But still a game old girl
(And I a game old guy) good
For a tumble in the August
Grass right at the center
Of the dream of a landscape

Till I see her glittering eye
Has taken this thought exactly
As the toad's tongue takes a fly

So that we laugh and the moment
Passes but Mrs Persepolis
As the bees go about their business
And we go in to have lunch
(How cold the house, the sudden
Shade! I shiver, and Mrs
Persepolis shivers too, till
Her bangles bangle) my dear
Mrs Persepolis, beautiful
Exile from childhood, girl
In your rough and wrinkled
Sack suit, couldn't you cry
Over that funny moment when
We almost fell together
Into the green sleep of the
Landscape, the hooded hills
That dream us up & down?

The Human Condition

In this motel where I was told to wait,
The television screen is stood before
The picture window. Nothing could be more
Use to a man than knowing where he's at,
And I don't know, but pace the day in doubt
Between my looking in and looking out.

Through snow, along the snowy road, cars pass
Going both ways, and pass behind the screen
Where heads of heroes sometimes can be seen
And sometimes cars, that speed across the glass.
Once I saw world and thought exactly meet,
But only in a picture by Magritte.

A picture of a picture, by Magritte,
Wherein a landscape on an easel stands
Before a window opening on a land-
scape, and the pair of them a perfect fit,
Silent and mad. You know right off, the room
Before that scene was always an empty room.

And that is now the room in which I stand
Waiting, or walk, and sometimes try to sleep.
The day falls into darkness while I keep
The TV going; headlights blaze behind
Its legendary traffic, love and hate,
In this motel where I was told to wait.

Beyond the Pleasure Principle

It comes up out of the darkness, and it returns
Into a further darkness. After the monster,
There is the monster's mother to be dealt with,
Dimly perceived at first, or only speculated on
Between the shadows and reflexions of the tidal cave,
Among the bones and armored emptiness
Of the princes of a former time, who failed.

Our human thought arose at first in myth,
And going far enough became a myth once more;
Its pretty productions in between, those splendid
Tarnhelms and winged sandals, mirroring shields
And swords unbreakable, of guaranteed
Fatality, those endlessly winding labyrinths
In which all minotaurs might find themselves at home,
Deceived us with false views of the end, leaving
Invisible the obstinate residuum, so cloudy, cold,
Archaic, that waits beyond purpose and fulfillment.

There, toward the end, when the left-handed wish
Is satisfied as it is given up, when the hero
Endures his cancer and more obstinately than ever
Grins at the consolations of religion as at a child's
Frightened pretensions, and when his great courage
Becomes a wish to die, there appears, so obscurely,
Pathetically, out of the wounded torment and the play,
A something primitive and appealing, and still dangerous,
That crawls on bleeding hands and knees over the floor
Toward him, and whispers as if to confess: *again, again.*

Christmas Morning

I snuggle down under the electric blanket
Turned onto high, and sneak a look at the dawn
With one pure fire of a sinking star
Over the gray snow blanketing the lawn;

Now once again the Child is born. Downstairs
The children are early out of bed, ready
To tear the wrappings from the usual junk
Where helpless love became commodity

As knowing nothing else to do. Downstreet
The lit-up crèche before the Baptist Church
Is lapped in filthy snow, its figures stained
And leaning at a hazard in the lurch

Of headstones heaved by frost; theirs is the strength
That makes the life-size plastic toy machine-
guns on which even a moment's happiness
Depends, with all the safety of the scene—

The whitened village on the greeting card
Sent by the Bank—against the alien priest
Who drenches his white robes in gasoline
And blazes merrily in the snowy East.

The Blue Swallows

Across the millstream below the bridge
Seven blue swallows divide the air
In shapes invisible and evanescent,
Kaleidoscopic beyond the mind's
Or memory's power to keep them there.

"History is where tensions were,"
"Form is the diagram of forces."
Thus, helplessly, there on the bridge,
While gazing down upon those birds—
How strange, to be above the birds!—
Thus helplessly the mind in its brain
Weaves up relation's spindrift web,
Seeing the swallows' tails as nibs
Dipped in invisible ink, writing . . .

Poor mind, what would you have them write?
Some cabalistic history
Whose authorship you might ascribe
To God? to Nature? Ah, poor ghost,
You've capitalized your Self enough.
That villainous William of Occam
Cut out the feet from under that dream
Some seven centuries ago.
It's taken that long for the mind
To waken, yawn and stretch, to see
With opened eyes emptied of speech
The real world where the spelling mind
Imposes with its grammar book

Unreal relations on the blue
Swallows. Perhaps when you will have

Fully awakened, I shall show you
A new thing: even the water
Flowing away beneath those birds
Will fail to reflect their flying forms,
And the eyes that see become as stones
Whence never tears shall fall gain.

O swallows, swallows, poems are not
The point. Finding again the world,
That is the point, where loveliness
Adorns intelligible things
Because the mind's eye lit the sun.

The Mud Turtle

Out of the earth beneath the water,
Dragging over the stubble field
Up to the hilltop in the sun
On his way from water to water,
He rests an hour in the garden,
His alien presence observed by all:
His lordly darkness decked in filth
Bearded with weed like a lady's favor,
He is a black planet, another world
Never till now appearing, even now
Not quite believably old and big,
Set in the summer morning's midst
A gloomy gemstone to the sun opposed.
Our measures of him do not matter,
He would be huge at any size;
And neither does the number of his years,
The time he comes from doesn't count.

When the boys tease him with sticks
He breaks the sticks, striking with
As great a suddenness as speed;
Fingers and toes would snap as soon,
Says one of us, and the others shudder.
Then when they turn him on his back
To see the belly heroically yellow,
He throws himself fiercely to his feet,
Brings down the whole weight of his shell,
Spreads out his claws and digs himself in
Immovably, invulnerably.

But for the front foot on the left,
Red-budded, with the toes torn off.
So over he goes again, and shows
Us where a swollen leech is fastened
Softly between plastron and shell.
Nobody wants to go close enough
To burn it loose; he can't be helped
Either, there is no help for him
As he makes it to his feet again
And drags away to the meadow's edge.
We see the tall grass open and wave
Around him, it closes, he is gone
Over the hill toward another water,
Bearing his hard and chambered hurt
Down, down, down, beneath the water,
Beneath the earth beneath. He takes
A secret wound out of the world.

Summer's Elegy

Day after day, day after still day,
The summer has begun to pass away.
Starlings at twilight fly clustered and call,
And branches bend, and leaves begin to fall.
The meadow and the orchard grass are mown,
And the meadowlark's house is cut down.

The little lantern bugs have doused their fires,
The swallows sit in rows along the wires.
Berry and grape appear among the flowers
Tangled against the wall in secret bowers,
And cricket now begins to hum the hours
Remaining to the passion's slow procession
Down from the high place and the golden session
Wherein the sun was sacrificed for us.
A failing light, no longer numinous,
Now frames the long and solemn afternoons
Where butterflies regret their closed cocoons.
We reach the place unripe, and made to know
As with a sudden knowledge that we go
Away forever, all hope of return
Cut off, hearing the crackle of the burn-
ing blade behind us, and the terminal sound
Of apples dropping on the dry ground.

For Robert Frost, in the Autumn, in Vermont

All on the mountains, as on tapestries
Reversed, their threads unreadable though clear,
The leaves turn in the volume of the year.
Your land becomes more brilliant as it dies.

The puzzled pilgrims come, car after car,
With cameras loaded for epiphanies;
For views of failure to take home and prize,
The dying tourists ride through realms of fire.

"To die is gain," a virgin's tombstone said;
That was New England, too, another age
That put a higher price on maidenhead
if brought in dead; now on your turning page
The lines blaze with a constant light, displayed
As in the maple's cold and fiery shade.

Firelight in Sunlight

Firelight in sunlight, silver-pale
Streaming with emerald, copper, sapphire
Ribbons and rivers, banners, fountains;
They rise, they run swiftly away.

Now apple logs unlock their sunlight
In the many-windowed room to meet
New sunlight falling in silvered gold
Through the fern-ice forest of the glass
Whose tropic surface light may pierce
If not the eye. O early world,
Still Daphne of the stubborn wood
Singing Apollo's song in light,
O pulsing constancies of flame
Warping a form along the log's
Slowly disintegrating face
Crackled and etched, so quickly aged,
These are my mysteries to see
And say and celebrate with words
In orders until now reserved.

For light is in the language now,
Carbon and sullen diamond break
Out of the glossary of earth
In holy signs and scintillations,
Release their fiery emblems to
Renewal's room and morning's room
Where sun and fire once again

Phase in the figure of the dance
From far beginnings here returned,
Leapt from the maze at the forest's heart,
O moment where the lost is found!

FROM

Gnomes and Occasions

1973

On Being a Member of the Jury
for a Poetry Prize

Jury's the *mot juste* under our ground rules:
I may say Guilty, and I mostly do,
But sentencing's beyond me, poeticules,
As, by your poems, it's beyond most of you.

September, the First Day of School

I

My child and I hold hands on the way to school,
And when I leave him at the first-grade door
He cries a little but is brave; he does
Let go. My selfish tears remind me how
I cried before that door a life ago.
I may have had a hard time letting go.

Each fall the children must endure together
What every child also endures alone:
Learning the alphabet, the integers,
Three dozen bits and pieces of a stuff
So arbitrary, so peremptory,
That worlds invisible and visible

Bow down before it, as in Joseph's dream
The sheaves bowed down and then the stars bowed down
Before the dreaming of a little boy.
That dream got him such hatred of his brothers
As cost the greater part of life to mend,
And yet great kindness came of it in the end.

II

A school is where they grind the grain of thought,
And grind the children who must mind the thought.
It may be those two grindings are but one,
As from the alphabet come Shakespeare's Plays,
As from the integers comes Euler's Law,
As from the whole, inseparably, the lives,

The shrunken lives that have not been set free
By law or by poetic phantasy.
But may they be. My child has disappeared
Behind the schoolroom door. And should I live
To see his coming forth, a life away,
I know my hope, but do not know its form

Nor hope to know it. May the fathers he finds
Among his teachers have a care of him
More than his father could. How that will look
I do not know, I do not need to know.
Even our tears belong to ritual.
But may great kindness come of it in the end.

After Commencement

Across the trampled, program-littered grass
A thousand yellow chairs have broken ranks
Before the ramrod silver microphone
That stands there on the platform unaddressed
And finished with the clichés of command.

O ceremony, ceremony! Let
Expression be the mere formality
The day demands; for emptiness alone
Has generality enough to send
Yet one more generation to the world,

And platitudes become the things they are
By being uninformative and true:
The words that for the hundredth time today
Bounced off the sunlit stone into the past
Have made the silence deeper by degrees.

On Being Asked for a Peace Poem

Here is Joe Blow the poet
Sitting before the console of the giant instrument
That mediates his spirit to the world.
He flexes his fingers nervously,
He ripples off a few scale passages
(Shall I compare thee to a summer's day?)
And resolutely readies himself to begin
His poem about the War in Vietnam.

This poem, he figures, is
A sacred obligation: all by himself,
Applying the immense leverage of art,
He is about to stop this senseless war.
So Homer stopped that dreadful thing at Troy
By giving the troops the Iliad to read instead;
So Wordsworth stopped the Revolution when
He felt that Robespierre had gone too far;
So Yevtushenko was invited in the *Times*
To keep the Arabs out of Israel
By smiting once again his mighty lyre.[1]
Joe smiles. He sees the Nobel Prize
Already, and the reading of his poem
Before the General Assembly, followed by
His lecture to the Security Council
About the Creative Process; probably
Some bright producer would put it on TV.
Poetry might suddenly be the in thing.

Only trouble was, he didn't have
A good first line, though he thought that for so great
A theme it would be right to start with O,
Something he would not normally have done,

O

And follow on by making some demands
Of a strenuous sort upon the Muse
Polyhymnia of Sacred Song, that Lady
With the fierce gaze and implacable small smile.

[1] "An Open Letter to Yevgeny Yevtushenko, Poet Extraordinary of
Humanity," advt., Charles Rubinstein, *New York Times*, November 3,
1966.

To D——, Dead by Her Own Hand

My dear, I wonder if before the end
You ever thought about a children's game—
I'm sure you must have played it too—in which
You ran along a narrow garden wall
Pretending it to be a mountain ledge
So steep a snowy darkness fell away
On either side to deeps invisible;
And when you felt your balance being lost
You jumped because you feared to fall, and thought
For only an instant: That was when I died.

That was a life ago. And now you've gone,
Who would no longer play the grown-ups' game
Where, balanced on the ledge above the dark,
You go on running and you don't look down,
Nor ever jump because you fear to fall.

The Beautiful Lawn Sprinkler

What gives it power makes it change its mind
At each extreme, and lean its rising rain
Down low, first one and then the other way;
In which exchange humility and pride
Reverse, forgive, arise, and die again,
Wherefore it holds at both ends of the day
The rainbow in its scattering grains of spray.

The Western Approaches

Einstein & Freud & Jack

to Allen Tate on his 75th Birthday

Death is a dead, at least that's what Freud said.
Long considering, he finally thought
Life but a detour longer or less long;
Maybe that's why the going gets so rough.

When Einstein wrote to ask him what he thought
Science might do for world peace, Freud wrote back:
Not much. And took the occasion to point out
That science too begins and ends in myth.

His myth was of the sons conspired together
To kill the father and share out his flesh,
Blood, power, women, and the primal guilt
Thereon entailed, which they must strive

Vainly to expiate by sacrifice,
Fixed on all generations since, of sons.
Exiled in London, a surviving Jew,
Freud died of cancer before the war began

That Einstein wrote to Roosevelt about
Advising the research be started that,
Come seven years of dying fathers, dying sons,
In general massacre would end the same.

Einstein. He said that if it were to do
Again, he'd sooner be a plumber. He

Died too. We live on sayings said in myths,
And die of them as well, or ill. That's that,

Of making many books there is no end,
And like it saith in the book before that one,
What God wants, don't you forget it, Jack,
Is your contrite spirit, Jack, your broken heart.

Wolves in the Zoo

They look like big dogs badly drawn, drawn wrong.
A legend on their cage tells us there is
No evidence that any of their kind
Has ever attacked man, woman, or child.

Now it turns out there were no babies dropped
In sacrifice, delaying tactics, from
Siberian sleds; now it turns out, so late,
That Little Red Ridinghood and her Gran

Were the aggressors with the slavering fangs
And tell-tale tails; now it turns out at last
That grey wolf and timber wolf are near extinct,
Done out of being by the tales we tell

Told us by Nanny in the nursery;
Young sparks we were, to set such forest fires
As blazed from story into history
And put such bounty on their wolvish heads

As brought the few survivors to our terms,
Surrendered in happy Babylon among
The peacock dusting off the path of dust,
The tiger pacing in the stripéd shade.

The Common Wisdom

Their marriage is a good one. In our eyes
What makes a marriage *good?* Well, that the tether
Fray but not break, and that they stay together.
One should be watching while the other dies.

The Dependencies

This morning, between two branches of a tree
Beside the door, epeira once again
Has spun and signed his tapestry and trap.
I test his early-warning system and
It works, he scrambles forth in sable with
The yellow hieroglyph that no one knows
The meaning of. And I remember now
How yesterday at dusk the nighthawks came
Back as they do about this time each year,
Grey squadrons with the slashes white on wings
Cruising for bugs beneath the bellied cloud.
Now soon the monarchs will be drifting south,
And then the geese will go, and then one day
The little garden birds will not be here.
See how many leaves already have
Withered and turned; a few have fallen, too.
Change is continuous on the seamless web,
Yet moments come like this one, when you feel
Upon your heart a signal to attend
The definite announcement of an end
Where one thing ceases and another starts;
When like the spider waiting on the web
You know the intricate dependencies
Spreading in secret through the fabric vast
Of heaven and earth, sending their messages
Ciphered in chemistry to all the kinds,
The whisper down the bloodstream: it is time.

A Cabinet of Seeds Displayed

These are the original monies of the earth,
In which invested, as the spark in fire,
They will produce a green wealth toppling tall,
A trick they do by dying, by decay,
In burial becoming each his kind
To rise in glory and be magnified
A million times above the obscure grave.

Reader, these samples are exhibited
For contemplation, locked in potency
And kept from act for reverence's sake.
May they remind us while we live on earth
That all economies are primitive;
And by their reservations may they teach
Our governors, who speak of husbandry
And think the hurricane, where power lies.

Again

Again, great season, sing it through again
Before we fall asleep, sing the slow change
That makes October burn out red and gold
And color bleed into the world and die,
And butterflies among the fluttering leaves
Disguise themselves until the few last leaves
Spin to the ground or to the skimming streams
That carry them along until they sink,
And through the muted land, the nevergreen
Needles and mull and duff of the forest floor,
The wind go ashen, till one afternoon
The cold snow cloud comes down the intervale
Above the river on whose slow black flood
The few first flakes come hurrying in to drown.

Near the Old People's Home

The people on the avenue at noon,
Sharing the sparrows and the wintry sun,
The turned-off fountain with its basin drained
And cement benches etched with checkerboards,

Are old and poor, most every one of them
Wearing some decoration of his damage,
Bandage or crutch or cane; and some are blind,
Or nearly, tap-tapping along with white wands.

When they open their mouths, there are no teeth.
All the same, they keep on talking to themselves
Even while bending to hawk up spit or blood
In gutters that will be there when they are gone.

Some have the habit of getting hit by cars
Three times a year; the ambulance comes up
And away they go, mumbling even in shock
The many secret names they have for God.

Conversing with Paradise

for Robert Jordan

To see the world the way a painter must,
Responsive to distances, alive to light,
To changes in the colors of the day,
His mind vibrating at every frequency
He finds before him, from wind waves in wheat
Through trees that turn their leaves before the storm,
To the string-bag pattern of the pebbled waves
Over the shallows of the shelving cove
In high sunlight; and to the greater wave-
lengths of boulder and building, to the vast
Majestic measures of the mountain's poise;

And from these modulations of the light
To take the elected moment, silence it
In oils and earths beneath the moving brush,
And varnish it and put it in a frame
To seal it off as privileged from time,
And hang it for a window on the wall,
A window giving on the ever-present past;

How splendid it would be to be someone
Able to do these mortal miracles
In silence and solitude, without a word.

An Ending

After the weeks of unrelenting heat
A rainy day brings August to an end
As if in ceremony. The spirit, dry
From too much light too steadily endured,
Delights in the heavy silver water globes
That make change from the sun's imperial gold;
The mind, relieved from being always brilliant,
Goes forth a penitent in a shroud of grey
To walk the sidewalks that reflect the sky,
The line of lights diminishing down the street,
The splashed lights of the traffic going home.

FROM

Sentences

1980

The Serial

The last year's phone books lying in the rain
With other garbage to be taken away
Are obsolescing programs that contain
The dramatis personae of a play
So vast its purposes and plot
Go ramifying out of mortal sight
In intricate radiations, rise and rot;
Here lie the yellow pages and the white,
Going concerns and bankrupt, where the dead
Hide with the living in the book of life,
The slowly moving serial unread
Whose singles with the husband and the wife
      Are persons parted, who as they leave the stage
      Get quietly stood in for, page by page.

Manners

Prig offered Pig the first chance at dessert,
So Pig reached out and speared the bigger part.

"Now that," cried Prig, "is extremely rude of you!"
Pig, with his mouth full, said, "Wha, wha' wou' 'ou do?"

"I would have taken the littler bit," said Prig.
"Stop kvetching, then it's what you've got," said Pig.

So virtue is its own reward, you see.
And that is all it's ever going to be.

Monet

Unable to get into the Monet show,
Too many people there, too many cars,
We spent the Sunday morning at Bowl Pond
A mile from the Museum, where no one was,
And walked an hour or so around the rim
Beside five acres of flowering waterlilies
Lifting three feet above their floating pads
Huge yellow flowers heavy on bending stems
In various phases of array and disarray
Of petals packed, unfolded, opening to show
The meaty orange centers that become,
When the ruined flags fall away, green shower heads
Spilling their wealth of seed at summer's end
Into the filthy water among small fish
Mud-colored and duck moving explorative
Through jungle pathways opened among the fronds
Upon whose surface water drops behave
Like mercury, collecting in heavy silver coins
Instead of bubbles; some few redwinged blackbirds
Whistling above all this once in a while,
The silence else unbroken all about.

Acorn, Yom Kippur

Look at this little fallen thing, it's got
Its yarmulka still on, and a jaunty sprig
Of a twig, a feather in its cap, and in its head
There is a single-minded thought: *White Oak.*

Language and thought have changed since I was young
And we used to say it had an oak inside,
The way some tribes believe that every man
Has a homunculus inside his head.
Already, though, matter was going out
And energy coming in; though energy
Wasn't the last word either, the last word
Is information, or, more tersely, The Word.
Inside its dreaming head the acorn has
Complete instructions for making an oak
Out of the sun and the local water and soil,
Not to forget the great stretches of time
Required for cracking the code, solving the script,
Translating the sacred book of the white oak
With its thousands of annual leaves and their footnotes
—Amounting to millions in a century—
Instructing the oak in the making of acorns
And so forth and so on, world without end.

What the moral of this may be I do not know.
But once a mystical lady in a dream
Beheld her Savior, an acorn in his hand,
And asking what might this be was answered thus:
"It is in a manner everything that is made."

Morning Glory

Convolvulus it's called as well, or ill,
And bindweed, though sweating gardeners
Believe it rightly christened The Devil's Guts.

After it's tied whole hedges up in knots
And strangled all the flowers in a bed
And started to ambition after trees,

It opens out its own pale trumpet-belled
Five-bladed blooms—from white of innocence
Shading to heavenly blue—so frail they fall
At almost a touch, and even left alone
        Endure but a day.

The Dying Garden

The flowers get a darkening brilliance now;
And in the still sun-heated air stand out
As stars and soloists where they had been before
Choruses and choirs; at the equinox,
I mean, when the great gyroscope begins
To spin the sun under the line and do
Harvest together with fall: the time that trees
Crimp in their steepled shapes, the hand of leaf
Become a claw; when wealth and death are one,
When moth and wasp and mouse come in the house
For comfort if they can; the deepening time
When sketchy Orion begins his slow cartwheel
About the southern sky, the time of turn
When moth and wasp and mouse come in the house
To die there as they may; and there will be,
You know, All Saints, All Souls, and Halloween,
The killing frost, the end of Daylight Time,
Sudden the nightfall on the afternoon
And on children scuffling home through drifts of leaf;
Till you drop the pumpkins on the compost heap,
The blackened jack o'lanterns with their candled eyes,
And in the darkening garden turn for home
Through summer's flowers now all gone, withdrawn,
The four o'clocks, the phlox, the hollyhocks,
Somber November in amber and umber embering out.

A Christmas Storm

All Sunday and Sunday night, cold water drops
At the will of heaven, freezing where it hits,
Glazing the windshields and the glistening ways,
Sheathing the branches and the power lines
In leaden insulations uniform
Across the counties and the towns, until
Connections loosen out and lines come down
And limbs that had sustained the horizontal
A hundred years unstrained crack under the weight
Of stiffened wet and short transformers out
So that ten thousand homes turned suddenly off
Go grey and silent, and the cold comes in
Slowly at first, then faster, drifting through
The window frames ghostly, under doors,
While night comes on and provident families
Remember where the candles and lanterns were
From last year, and other families don't;
While lucky families light fires, and others can't
But bundle up in blankets or skid downstreet
To the kindness of their neighbors or their kin,
And cars caught out are paralyzed at hills,
And it is clear that the relentless rain
Will go unrelentingly on till it relents:

Which it does do only next day at dawn,
When sunrise summons up the pride of the eye
To radiant brocades of fabergé'd
Drainpipes and eaves and scintillant fans
Of bush and tree turned emblems of themselves;

Where every twig is one and three, itself,
Its chrysalis in ice transparent, and last
Haloed in splintering light, as in the great
Museum of mind the million Christmas trees
Illuminate their diamonded display
To crystalline magnificent candelabra
Of silver winking ruby and emerald and gold
As angled to the sun by the glittering wind,
To show forth, to show up, to show off
The rarely tinselled treasures of the world
Before the powerful, before the poor.

Easter

Even this suburb has overcome Death.
Overnight, by a slow explosion, or
A rapid burning, it begins again
Bravely disturbing the brown ground
With grass and even more elaborate
Unnecessaries such as daffodils
And tulips, till the whole sordid block
Of houses turned so inward on themselves,
So keeping of a winter's secret sleep,
Looks like a lady's hat, improbably
Nodding with life, with bluejays hooting
And pigeons caracoling up among
The serious chimney pots, and pairs
Of small birds speeding behind the hedges
Readying to conceal them soon. Here,
Even here, Death has been vanquished again,
What was a bramble of green barbed wire
Becomes forsythia, as the long war
Begins again, not by our doing or desiring.

By Al Lebowitz's Pool

I

Imagine this: three beach balloons of three
Sizes, sometimes spinning and sometimes not,
Float in the transparent water table
Reflecting light blue light up from the floor.
They slightly sink into their own images
Mirrored below themselves as bubbles a bit
Elongate gaining and losing their various colors
According as they move between sun and shade,
Shade of the sailing cloud, shade of the oak
And sycamore and apple standing over
Or bending above, and through the dappled light
Respondingly they drift before light airs,
Sailing in independence that is yet
Relation, unpredictable if not
Quite free, mysteriously going about
Their balancing buoyancies sometimes puffed
On some bits of V-shaped wake; like a mobile
By Calder, only more so—linkages
Invisible, of wind and the watching mind,
Connect and vary their free-hand forms. The world
Is a misery, as it always was; these globes
Of color bob about, a mystery
Of pure relation that looks always right
Whatever it does. A steel-blue-black wasp
Rides on one ball awhile, flies to the next,
Possibly playing, possibly not; by law

Any three things in the wide world
Triangulate: the wasp, and Betelgeuse,
And Our Lady of Liberty in the harbor; if
It's any comfort to us, and it is.

II

Sunshine and rain at once, and the clear pool
At once lights up its light and shadow show,
Doing its free-hand random perfect circles
That on a nucleus of bubble and drop
Grow outward and silently intersect
Without collision or consequence, as if
They lived between the spirit and the world,
And evanescing are replaced by others
In patterns that repeat themselves beneath
In light and shade that seem to ripple away
Between the surface and the floor and dazzle
Again against the sunshine side. Dame Kind
Is doing one of her mighty and meaningless
Experimental demonstrations, but
Of What? Playing, perhaps, with the happiness of
A couple of groups of aperiodic crystals
Like thee and me, who are old enough to know
That if these moments could not pass away
They could not be, all dapple and delight.

III

Two girls in the pool, two old men out of it
Observing with an implicit kind of love
Mildly distinguished from lechery, much from lust,
The slender strong young bodies sudden as fish
To dive and swerve in the dazzled element
And surface (no longer much like fish at all)
Smiling, their long hair asparkle as with stars.
The old men, relaxed into their middle ages
And comfortable in the flesh for yet awhile,
Whom generation has had its will and fill of
And nearly if not quite let go, smile back
Over their drinks and banter with the girls
In a style that allows courtship and courtesy
To show their likenesses and keep their distance,
Just glancingly at risk; and the young women
Kindly respond in kind. No one, praise God,
Is going to get in trouble this time around.
It is late Sunday morning by the pool,
A Sunday morning late in summer time
A Sunday morning of the middle class,
And no one, praise God, is even like to drown
Before it's time to go indoors for lunch.

IV

Likely the last of the summer's storms goes by,
And even the water in the pool looks lank,
With leaves already dead upon its flat
Spinning a while and sinking waterlogged,

A couple of struggling bugs doing the same.
Even the heat begins to ember out,
The year has perceptibly started down again,
And summer's wondering stillness is on the move
Over ourselves as well; a leaf comes down
And alights without a splash; another year
Of the little lot has passed, and what have we
Squirreled away more than this summer's day
With the electric storm hammering down on it
Releasing life? The banked furnace of the sun
With reliquary heat returns in splendor
Diminished some with time, but splendid still.
Beside the pool we drink, talk, and are still,
These times of kindness mortality allows.

V

An afternoon alone beside the pool
Observing, or more like peaceably taking in,
Recording, stillness made of rippling wave
And waving leaf, of shadow and reflected light,
And silence able to draw into its dream
The siren singing on the avenue,
The crying of a child two houses down,
The aircraft laboring through four thousand feet
On the way elsewhere. Stillness and silence still,
Shimmering frequencies of waterlight
Reflected from the planes of leaf above
And from the screening panels of the pool,
So many white oscilloscopes whereon
The brimming water translates into light.

Reflection and reflexion, lovely words
I shall be sorry to let go when I let go:
Reflected light, reflexion of the wave;
For things reflected are more solemn and still
Than in themselves they are, it is the doubling
Perhaps that seems to bring them nearer thought;
Could we reflect, did water not reflect?

Enchanted afternoon, immune from time,
Illusion's privilege gives me the idea that I
Am not so much writing this verse as reading it
Up out of water and light and shadow and leaf
Doing the dance of their various dependencies—
As if I might daydream my way again
Into the world and be at one with it—
While the shadows of harder, more unyielding things
Edge steadily and stealthily around the pool
To translate the revolving of the world
About itself, the spinning ambit of the seasons
In the simple if adamant equation of time
Around the analemma of the sun.

Because You Asked about the Line between Prose and Poetry

Sparrows were feeding in a freezing drizzle
That while you watched turned into pieces of snow
Riding a gradient invisible
From silver aslant to random, white, and slow.

There came a moment that you couldn't tell.
And then they clearly flew instead of fell.

FROM

Inside the Onion

1984

A Sprig of Dill

Small, fragrant, green, a stalk splits at the top
And rays out a hemisphere of twenty stems
That split in their turn and ray out twenty more
In hemispheres of twenty yellow stars
Targeted white, sprays mothered of spray
Displaying their tripled oneness all at once,
Radiant and delicate and loosely exact
As the cosmos in *The Comedy*, or as
The Copernican system on an orrery,
The quiet flowerworks of the mind of God
In an Age of Reason—that's in here. Out there,
The formless furnaces in Andromeda,
Hydra, The Veil, Orion's nightmare head.

Wintering

A prism hung in a window to the south
Spangles the room, the kitchen, the hall beyond,
With rainbows from the time of Orion's rise
Until the sun climbs up so high in May
His angle gets too thin to manage anything
More than a splinter of spectrum on the floor
Beneath the sill; but who needs rainbows then,
With the sun his radiant self all summer long?

No diamond from deep earth could celebrate
So well our long engagement with the world
As faceted glass dangled against the pane
To swing advantage from the sun's long swing
Low through the darkness and the burning cold
Until, sweet chariot, he brings us up
Again, poking the crocus through the snow
Again, and once more turns might into may.

Fish Swimming amid Falling Flowers

comme le pan de mur jaune que peignit avec tant de science
et de raffinement un artiste à jamais inconnu, à peine identifié . . .

On a ground of pale gold water of watered silk
The painter of a thousand years ago
Angled his wrist so rapidly and right
The hairs of the brush bent in obedience
To do the swerve and diagonal of these fish
Swimming in space, in water, on watered silk,
And stippled in the detail of their scales,
The pale translucency of tail and fin,
And dotted at the brush's very tip
The falling petals and the petals fallen,
And scattered a few lotus and lily pads
Across the surface of the watered silk
Whose weave obedient took all this in,
The surface petal-flat, the fish beneath
The golden water of the watered silk,

So that a thousand years of the world away
On this millennially distant shore of time
The visitor to the museum may stare
Bemused down through the glass hermetic seal
At the silken scroll still only half unrolled
Past centuries invisible as air
To where the timeless, ageless fish still swim,
And read the typescript on the card beside
That says "Fish Swimming Amid Falling Flowers"
A thousand years ago, and seeing agree

That carp did always swim, and always will,
In just that way, with just that lightning sweep
Of eye, wrist, brush across the yielding silk
Stretched tight with surface tension as the pool
Of pale gold water, pale gold watered silk.

The Air Force Museum at Dayton

Under the barrel roof in solemn gloom
The weapons, instruments, and winged shapes,
The pictured dead in period costume,
Illustrate as in summary time-lapse

Photography the planetary race
That in the span of old men still around
Arose from Kitty Hawk to sky to space,
Cooped up as if it never left the ground.

After the pterodactyl and the Wright
Brothers every kite carries a gun
As it was meant to do, for right and might
Are properly understood by everyone.

Destructive powers, and speeds still unforeseen
But half a life ago, stand passive here,
Contraptions that have landed on the Moon
Or cancelled cities in a single flare.

When anything's over, it turns into art,
Religion, history; what's come to pass
Bows down the mind and presses upon the heart:
The ancient bombsight here enshrined in glass

Is the relic left us of a robot saint
With a passion for accuracy, who long ago
Saw towns as targets miniature and quaint,
Townsfolk invisible that far below.

FROM

War Stories

1987

On an Occasion of National Mourning

It is admittedly difficult for a whole
Nation to mourn and be seen to do so, but
It can be done, the silvery platitudes
Were waiting in their silos for just such
An emergent occasion, cards of sympathy
From heads of state were long ago prepared
For launching and are bounced around the world
From satellites at near the speed of light,
The divine services are telecast
From the home towns, children are interviewed
And say politely, gravely, how sorry they are,

And in a week or so the thing is done,
The sea gives up its bits and pieces and
The investigating board pinpoints the cause
By inspecting bits and pieces, nothing of the sort
Can ever happen again, the prescribed course
Of tragedy is run through omen to amen
As in a play, the nation rises again
Reborn of grief and ready to seek the stars;
Remembering the shuttle, forgetting the loom.

Models

I

The boy of twelve, shaping a fuselage
Of balsa wood so easy to be sliced
Along the grain but likely to get crushed
Under the razor when it was cut across;

Sanding the parts, glueing and lacquering
And pasting on the crosses and the rings
The brave identities of Fokker and Spad
That fought, only a little before his birth,

That primitive, original war in the air
He made in miniature and flew by hand
In clumsy combat, simulated buzz:
A decade away from being there himself.

II

The fuselage in the factory was aligned on North
So that the molecules lay along the axis,
Or so they said, to make the compass read
A right magnetic course; and after an attack

You headed the aircraft to what you hoped was North
And fired one more burst at the empty night
To set the shaken compass true again:
It straightened the molecules, or so they said.

The broken circle with the centered cross
Projecting the image at infinity
Quivered before him in the vacant air
Till it lay on the target like a haloing light.

III

And memory, that makes things miniature
And far away, and fit size for the mind,
Returned him in the form of images
The size of flies, his doings in those days

With theirs, the heroes that came out of the sun
To invent the avant-garde war of the air—
Richtofen, Rickenbacker, and the rest—
Where if you were shot it would be in the back,

Where the survivors, by their likenesses
Before and after, aged decades in a year,
Cruel-mouthed and harsh, and thought the young recruit
Not worth their welcome, as unlike to last.

Night Operations, Coastal Command RAF

Remembering that war, I'd near believe
We didn't need the enemy, with whom
Our dark encounters were confused and few
And quickly done, so many of our lot
Did for themselves in folly and misfortune.

Some hit our own barrage balloons, and some
Tripped over power lines, coming in low;
Some swung on takeoff, others overshot,
And two or three forgot to lower the wheels.

There were those that flew the bearing for the course
And flew away forever; and the happy few
That homed on Venus sinking beyond the sea
In fading certitude. For all the skill,
For all the time of training, you might take
The hundred steps in darkness, not the next.

The War in the Air

For a saving grace, we didn't see our dead,
Who rarely bothered coming home to die
But simply stayed away out there
In the clean war, the war in the air.

Seldom the ghosts came back bearing their tales
Of hitting the earth, the incompressible sea,
But stayed up there in the relative wind,
Shades fading in the mind,

Who had no graves but only epitaphs
Where never so many spoke for never so few:
Per ardua, said the partisans of Mars,
Per aspera, to the stars.

That was the good war, the war we won
As if there were no death, for goodness' sake,
With the help of the losers we left out there
In the air, in the empty air.

The Afterlife

The many of us that came through the war
Unwounded and set free in Forty-Five
Already understood the afterlife
We'd learned enough to wait for, not expect,
During the years of boredom, fear, fatigue;
And now, an hour's worth of afterlife.

Fort Dix, there at the gate, boarding the bus
That let me off in Newark to catch a train
That took me to Penn Station and left me there
Once more the young man on his own and free
Without much money, and with not much to do:
The Gates of Paradise opened and let me out.

In the real one, as I understand it now,
They'll take you to a base camp far from home
And line you up for uniforms and shots
And scream incomprehensible commands
Until you learn obedience again.
It will feel strange at first. But so it goes.

On Reading *King Lear* Again, 1984

After the many things it's been about,
Maybe the one last thing *King Lear*'s about
Is God's way with his people and the world.

The white-haired widower's classic double-bind,
"How much do you love me?" against "I want the truth,"
Where flattery is required and the truth outlawed,

Is like the prayer demanded of the prey,
"Now tell me what you really think of me,
Before I kill you anyhow." Critics

Who cast Cordelia as "a type of Christ"
Should honor the obligation they incur
To all the story, not just part of it.

The god who gives the world away to kids
Will go a long road and a rainy night
Before his wits give way and he forgives.

FROM

Trying Conclusions

1991

To the Congress of the United States,
Entering Its Third Century

because reverence has never been america's thing,
       this verse in your honor will not begin "o thou."
but the great respect our country has to give
may you all continue to deserve, and have.

     *   *   *

here at the fulcrum of us all,
the feather of truth against the soul
is weighed, and had better be found to balance
lest our enterprise collapse in silence.

for here the million varying wills
get melted down, get hammered out
until the movie's reduced to stills
that tell us what the law's about.

conflict's endemic in the mind:
your job's to hear it in the wind
and compass it in opposites,
and bring the antagonists by your wits

to being one, and that the law
thenceforth, until you change your minds
against and with the shifting winds
that this and that way blow the straw.

so it's a republic, as Franklin said,
if you can keep it; and we did

thus far, and hope to keep our quarrel
funny and just, though with this moral:—

praise without end for the go-ahead zeal
of whoever it was invented the wheel;
but never a word for the poor soul's sake
that thought ahead, and invented the brake.

26 ii 89

Answering Back

"Does the imagination dwell the most
Upon a woman won or a woman lost?"

—W. B. Yeats

You silly Willie, on the woman lost.
The woman won sits in the inglenook
Across from you, knitting or reading a book
Or come your teatime doing the toast and bacon;
Whereas the woman lost is God knows where
In the world, and with whom, if not by now a ghost
Past yours or anyone's love, though still you care
Lest she be by another bespoken or taken—
For what's romantic love unless forsaken?

Larkin

Imagine Larkin going among the dead,
Not yet at home there, as he wasn't here,
And doing them the way he did *The Old Fools,*
With edged contempt becoming sympathy
Of a sort, and sympathy contempt for death.

It's a quirky spirit he carried through the arch
To aftertime, making a salted fun
Of all the show and grudging his respect
For all but truth, the master of a style
Able to see things as he saw through things.

He was our modern; in his attitude,
And not in all that crap about free verse.
He understood us, not as we would be
Understood in smartass critical remarks,
But as we are when we stand in our shoes and say.

Our Roman, too; he might not have cared to be,
But what I mean is this: you wander through
The galleries entranced with shepherdess and nymph,
The marble or alabaster faery and fay,
Then suddenly you come on him, the stone

Of his face scored up and scarred with the defeat
An honorable life has brought him to,
And know that backing up the tales we tell
Is mortal this, the what-it's-all-about,
So that you turn away, the lesson told,

That's it. Dear Warlock-Williams, might you weep?
The penetrative emptiness of that gaze
Kindly accusing none, forgiving none,
Is just the look upon the face of truth,
Mortality knowing itself as told to do,

And death the familiar comes as no surprise—
"Ah, Warlock-Williams, are you here as well?"
With Auden, with Hardy, with the other great and dead,
Dear Larkin of the anastrophic mind,
Forever now among the undeceived.

The Forbidden City

When the youths and maidens had been sacrificed
And their burned bodies bundled away by night,
The mediate mind erased their images,
Replacing what the witnesses said they saw
With memories preferred by the regime.

The world well knew it listened to a lie
Made up of lies, but nodded its great head
Globular and said it was the way of the world
To know the truth and prefer to be deceived,
Smoothed over and soothed in cynical innocence,

No matter what Cassandra cried, whose curse
Was to tell the truth and never be believed;
One hand will wash the other, never mind
If waterish indifference disregard
What resentment implacable bakes sour and hard.

The End of the Opera

to Mona Van Duyn

Knowing that what he witnessed was only art,
He never wept while the show was going on.

But the curtain call could always make him cry.
When the cast came forward hand in hand
Bowing and smiling to the clatter of applause,
Tired, disheveled, sweating through the paint,
Radiant with our happiness and theirs,
Illuminati of the spot and flood,
Yet much the same as ordinary us.

The diva, the soubrette, the raisonneur,
The inadequate hero, the villain, his buffoon,
All equalled in the great reality
And living proof that life would follow life . . .

Though back of that display there'd always be,
He knew, money and envy, the career,
Tomorrow and tomorrow—it didn't seem
At that moment as if it mattered much
Compared with their happiness and ours
As we wept about the role, about the real,
And how their dissonances harmonized
As we applauded us: *ite, missa est.*

Trying Conclusions

I

There is a punishment too smart for Hell,
And it is this: some people here on earth
Have been so hot at prayer that when they come
At last to bliss eternal they cannot stop
Blessing, beseeching, praising His Holy Name.

They would spend eternity hunkered on their knees
Without a cushion, save that the Infinite
Of wisdom and mercy pities them in the end.
They are the ones He will send to be born again.

II

What rational being, after seventy years,
When Scripture says he's running out of rope,
would want more of the only world he knows?

No rational being, he while he endures
Holds on to the inveterate infantile hope
That the road ends but as the runway does.

Index of Titles and First Lines